History
of

The Sagamore Hotel

William Preston Gates

© W. P. Gates Publishing Company

> Dedicated to —
> ## Dawn, my mother.
> Thank you for your part in teaching me to
> appreciate and enjoy our local history.

Published by:
W. P. GATES Publishing Company
William P. Gates
1 Glenwood Avenue
Queensbury, NY 12804
(518) 798-3609
• or •
Box 405
Bolton Landing, NY 12814
(518) 644-9410

Library of Congress Control No. 2001116568
ISBN #0-9672397-2-9 (Softcover)

Front Cover Design: William P. Gates
Front Cover Photo of First Sagamore 1883 - 1893: Jules A. Thatcher
Front Cover Photo of Present Sagamore: Richard K. Dean
Technical Assistant: Donnaleen E. Hoffman

During the summer of 2001, Mark Frost and the Chronicle newspaper published one photograph each week to publicize this book. All of the published photographs are included in this book which contains over 260 historic photographs and sketches.

Foreword

The Sagamore Hotel on Lake George in Bolton Landing, New York, has appeared in pages and chapters of numerous books and publications from 1883 to the present day, however, there has never been an entire book devoted to this magnificent hotel and its history.

With every passing year, significant information becomes lost and rare photographs gradually fade until their historic details are no longer easily distinguishable. Furthermore, the rare photographs and historic archives used to compile this book are separated around the region in museums, libraries and private collections.

By assembling this fascinating history between the protective covers of this book, I receive great pleasure in knowing that the "History of the Sagamore Hotel" will be forever available for present and future generations to preserve, appreciate and enjoy.

William P. Gates

WHITE BIRCH GROVE, GREEN ISLAND, LAKE GEORGE.

The Sagamore, Green Island, Lake George, season 1894, by M.O. Brown.
(Author's Collection)

4

$\mathcal{A}$cknowledgements

A successful book is the work of many people besides the author. This book would not be possible without the help of the following individuals and organizations who have provided me access to their skills, collections, photographs and information. For their direct involvement in the making and marketing of this book, and in no particular order, I sincerely wish to thank: — Director Pat Babé and The Bolton Historical Museum, Gordon Garlick for his extensive collection of Sagamore information and for all of the time he spends discussing history with me, Hugh Allen Wilson for his wonderful photos of Villa Nirvana, Bolton Town Historian Pat Steele, Gardner Finley, Jane Gabriels, Megan Brown and The Bolton Free Library, Henry Caldwell and Black Bass Antiques, Ike Wolgin, Ted Caldwell, Doug Houghton, Rebecca Pelchar and The Chapman Historical Museum, Mark Frost and The Chronicle, Jim LaVere, Marie Ellsworth and the Caldwell-Lake George Library, Jane O'Connell & Hildie Monroe and The Hillview Free Library, Dick and Mary Kowell, Evelyn Hersh, Dorothy Meyer Craig, Jim Marshall and The Post-Star, Bob Bayle, Bill Morgan, Dick Dean and Dean Studios, Albert Fowler and the Crandall Public Library, Robert McIntosh and The Sagamore Hotel, Tom Smack and the Sagamore Golf Course, Cornelia Wells and Trees Giftshop, Elsie Baldwin, Ted Rehm, Wesley Huck Jr., Leon Chase, Don Cornell, The Lake George Mirror, The Warrensburg News, Dave Ofiara and the Adirondack Community College Library, Marilyn VanDyke, Theta Curri, Ross French, Chuck Benoit and Coneco Lithographics, my friends at The Lake George Steamboat Company, my friends in Bolton and around the Lake George region, and my family for their encouragement and support: Bus and Dawn Gates Macey, Mike Gates, Allison Gates, Bud & Toni Gates, Jeanine & Sam Garnsey, Ryan Gates, Lindsey Gates, Alice Ackary, Sarah Combs, Clifford Gates, Bobby Gates, Barbara M. Gates, Peggy Harris Nobles and Barbara Gates Lawrence.

When the time finally arrived for me to commit my writing, photographs and page designs onto the computer, I was very fortunate to have Donnie Hoffman as my Technical Assistant. For hours, days and months, she skillfully applied her technical skills which gave visual life to the pages in my imagination.

GREEN ISLAND

Printed by Coneco Lithographics

Table of Contents

Foreword .... Page 3

Acknowledgements .... Page 4

Introduction .... Page 7

Early History of Green Island .... Page 9
• Indians • Father Isaac Jogues • French and Indian War
• Revolutionary War • Early land transactions.

The First "Cottages" and Their Owners .... Page 11
• E.B. Warren, p.12 • G. Burnham, p.14
• W. Bement, p.16 • J. B. Simpson, p.17.

The First Sagamore Hotel 1882-1893 .... Page 23
• Construction, p.26 • Interior, p.39 • Golf, p.42
• Docks, p.45 • Burns, p.48.

The Second Sagamore Hotel 1894-1914 .... Page 53
• Construction, p.54 • Interior, p.59 • Amusements, p.66 • Golf, p.67
• Docks, p.69 • Regattas, p.73 • Burns, p.78 • 1914 Races, p.81.

The Third (Present) Sagamore Hotel .... Page 83
• Later Cottages, p.85 • "Club" Construction, p.87
• Hotel Construction, p.92 • Golf, p.93 • Horse Shows, p.97
• Gold Cup Races, p.98 • Interior, p.104 • After WWII, p.106
• Governor's Conference, p.109 • DEC, p.112
• 1981 Sale & Renovation, p.113 • "The Morgan" p.115.

Epilogue .... Page 121

Bibliography .... Page 122

Sagamore Hotel on Lake George
1899

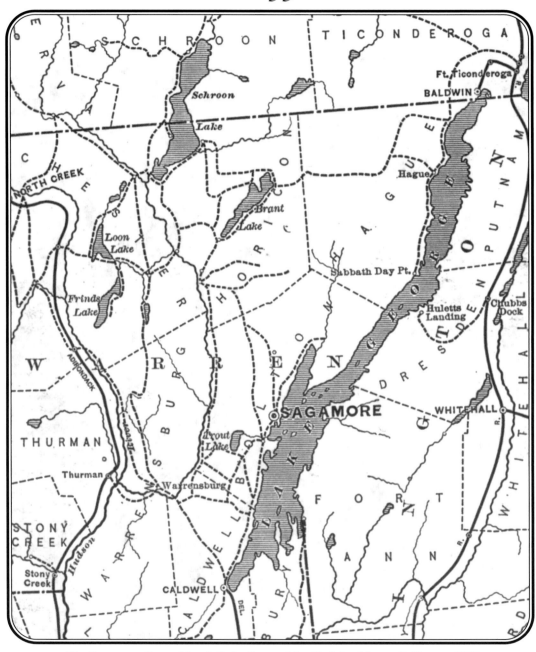

The Sagamore, Green Island, Lake George, New York, by Myron O. Brown, 1899.
(Courtesy, Bolton Town Historian)

$\mathcal{I}$ntroduction

When the Revolutionary War ended in 1783, a small handful of early pioneers began settling along the shores of Lake George. They were attracted to this new frontier by its beauty, and most importantly, by its bountiful opportunities. There was excellent hunting and fishing, and the rolling hills provided many satisfactory locations for farming, lumbering and the grazing of cattle.

The Great Chief "Sagamore"

By 1800, temporary summer visitors began arriving to enjoy their vacation time by camping among Lake George's nearly 200 islands. Those original tourist adventurers were primarily men from the eastern cities who were intent upon catching the largest fish or hunting down the mightiest deer. When they returned home, they told stories of their exploits on one of the most beautiful lakes they had ever explored.

The Sagamore on Lake George,
T.E. Krumbholz.
(Courtesy, Bolton Historical Museum)

As the summer tourist population increased, early local entrepreneurs began offering rooms for rent. Soon, small hotels began springing up along the lake's entire 32 miles. The first hotel in Bolton was the Mohican House on Mohican Point. Built in 1800, it survived for exactly 100 years before it was torn down to accommodate today's William K. Bixby mansion.

During the 1800's, finery and services were gradually added at the local hotels to attract female guests and couples. By the 1880's, opulence became the goal in the most strategic lakeside locations.

A favored site for the lakeshore hotels was one which commanded spectacular views while also offering convenient access for travelers. The southern point of Green Island in Bolton Landing was the ideal location for constructing a luxurious inn, —— and the magnificent hotel constructed there became known as ——

$\mathcal{T}he$ $\mathcal{S}agamore.$

LAKE FRONT, GREEN ISLAND, LAKE GEORGE.

The Sagamore, Green Island, Lake George, season 1894, by M.O. Brown.
(Author's Collection)

Early History of Green Island

(From Indians to 1881)

For centuries, the Indians of the Northeast roamed this region during the summer months to hunt, fish and explore. For protection and convenience, they camped in strategic locations around the lake which they affectionately called, "An-Di-A-Ta-Roc-Te," which translates to — "Where the mountains touch the water", or "Lake that shuts itself in." Undoubtedly, Green Island was one of their favored encampments as evidenced by the arrowheads and other Indian artifacts discovered there over the past two centuries.

In 1646, Father Isaac Jogues, a Jesuit missionary sent here by the French to convert the Eastern Indians to Christianity, named the lake — "Lac du Saint Sacrement", (Lake of the Blessed Sacrement), when he first arrived here on May 30, the eve of the Festival of Corpus Christi.

During the French and Indian War of 1754 - 1763, many battles occurred between the French and the English over control of this strategic water highway. During the construction of Fort William Henry in 1775, the British General, Sir William Johnson, named the lake, "Lake George", to honor his English King, a name which still stands today. During 1757, the French General Marquis de Montcalm paddled along the shores of Green Island with six thousand French regulars and two thousand Indians to attack and burn Fort William Henry, a story made famous in James Fenimore Cooper's novel, "The Last of the Mohicans". Major General James Abercrombie allegedly established a British headquarters on Green Island during 1758.

Lake George played an important part in the Revolutionary War as well. General Henry Knox hauled many of the cannon from Fort Ticonderoga past Green Island during the winter of 1775 - 1776 on his journey to Cambridge to help fortify Boston against the British. The 1861 French's Gazetteer states that: "During the Revolution, this (Green) Island was fortified, and General Burgoyne, when he advanced to the Hudson, left upon it a large amount of public property, guarded by two companies of the 6th Regiment, commanded by Captain Aubrey. After the attempt upon Ticonderoga in 1777, Warren and Brown, on the 24th of September, made an attack upon this place with the gunboats they had captured. They were repudiated with loss, and returned to the East shore. The enemy being in pursuit, they burned their boats, crossed the mountains to Lake Champlain, and returned to General Lincoln's camp at Pawlet, Vermont." In the final year of the Revolution, General George Washington inspected Lake George as did Thomas Jefferson. In a letter to his daughter, Jefferson glowingly described Lake George as, "The most beautiful water I ever saw."

After the Revolution, New York Governor George Clinton conveyed Green Island from the, "people of the State of New York", to "Wheeler Douglas", a Revolutionary War Veteran, on April 18, 1794. It later passed on to Jeremiah Van Rensselaer, and in 1842, a farmer purchased the whole island for $650. On June 15, 1847, it was purchased by Jacob Vandenburgh. John and Jacob Vandenburgh were known to have used the island for grazing their Hershey cattle during the summer months when the lush vegetation was at its thickest. They carried the cattle to the island on rafts. The only structure there at that time was a small shack. The island was covered then with a dense forest of deciduous trees, hemlocks and giant spruce.

It is recorded in 1855 that Ferdinand Theriot and James Buchanan Henry purchased the nearly 70 acres of land on the island for the sum of $600. In 1868, the island was surveyed, and Theriot and Henry each owned equal sized lots. In 1870, Mr. Theriot built a small home there, the first house built on Green Island. Later, it was moved down by the bridge and was occupied at various times by Fred W. Allen, George S. Gates, James Brown, William McCormack, Captain Clarence E. Wilson, and Arthur Bradley. After it was moved, porches were added. This home still stands today next to the Reception and Registration Building.

Private Residence Today.

First house on Green Island. Built in 1870, and here being renovated after it was moved down by the bridge. (Courtesy, Bolton Historical Museum)

The First Cottages and Their Owners

In 1881, Myron O. Brown, manager of the Mohican House in Bolton Landing, was ready for a change. Among his wealthy summer guests were four highly successful businessmen: E. Burgess Warren, William B. Bement, Robert Glendenning and George Burnham. Warren, Bement, and Burnham were from Philadelphia. Glendenning was from Glens Falls.

M.O. Brown, a Boltonian, convinced these gentleman to invest in Green Island, to construct a magnificent hotel there and to appoint him as General Manager. Theriot's half was purchased for $10,000 and Henry's half was purchased later for $20,000. Together, they formed the Green Island Improvement Company in 1881. Soon thereafter, a fifth wealthy investor joined the group — John Boulton Simpson of New York City.

The first of three bridges was built from the mainland to the island in 1882. This necessary connecting structure was constructed of logs and stonework, and it remained in use for fourteen years.

First Bridge, 1882.
(Courtesy, Bolton Historical Museum)

Before Bridge, 1881.
(Courtesy, Bolton Town Historian)

Four mansions, or "Cottages" as they were labeled, were constructed on the southern shores of Green Island after 1882. On the east side of the southern point was Commodore E. Burgess Warren's "Wapanak". His wealth was acquired in Philadelphia through his successful business, The Warren Roofing Company. Wapanak's stonework on the north side of the mansion resembles a medieval castle. E.B. Warren loved Lake George and spent most of his time out on the water, boating and fishing. The Lake George Mirror in 1892 states that he, "goes fishing before break-fast, and lives, eats, and almost sleeps on the water." The Mirror states again on August 13, 1898 that, "Mr. E. Burgess Warren made several catches of bass last week. One catch weighed 37

Early Wapanak. (Courtesy, Bolton Historical Museum)

pounds dressed, not including nine that were eaten at luncheon on board the boat." The Glens Falls Times for September 19, 1905 also states that Commodore Warren had, "retired from business during the panic of 1873 to become — *a fisherman.*" Warren's friends often joked that, "he hypnotised the bass". The caption on the photo of the bass on the right states, "caught by E.B. Warren, G. Halsey, Capt. Tailor, steam yacht Ellide, Sept. 7, 1898, whole catch weigh 42 1/4 lb."

Sagamore, Green Island, 1899, M.O. Brown. (Courtesy, Bolton Town Historian)

Warren's private yacht was called the "Ellide". As a founding member of the Lake George (Yacht) Club, he wanted to own the fastest steam yacht on the lake— and to his own surprise the Ellide was clocked in 1898 as the fastest boat in the world, at 40.2 mph. The Ellide's captain was George B. Harris.

(Left) *"Ellide"* — decorated for a regatta in front of Wapanak. Black Mountain and Shelving Rock visible.
(Courtesy, Hugh Allen Wilson)

(Right) *"Ellide"* — 40.2 mph, Fastest boat on Lake George — Fastest boat in the world.
Lake George and Surroundings, 1900, by W. H. Tippetts. (Author's Collection)

"Wapanak", means *People of the Morning*. Now on the National Register of Historic Places, it still stands proudly today. (Photo by Author.)

"East Cottage", owned by George Burnham, was located directly south of Wapanak. Of unique design, and constructed entirely of wood, it boasted many small covered porches facing all four directions around the cottage. Each porch had oval openings, picking up the nautical theme, by resembling large portholes.

"East Cottage" – *The Sagamore, Lake George,* 1895. M.O. Brown. (Author's Collection)

George Burnham

George Burnham's "East Cottage". (Courtesy, Bolton Historical Museum)

"East Cottage" and "Wapanak". (Author's Collection)

"East Cottage" and "Wapanak". (Courtesy, Bolton Historical Museum)

Both East Cottage and Wapanak shared a lakeside dock complex accessed by crossing an arched bridge constructed so that small boats could pass beneath it. East Cottage went into disrepair and was torn down and burned in the 1960's to open up the view from the Sagamore Hotel to the islands in the Narrows.

The Sagamore, 1893, M.O. Brown. (Author's Collection)

"East Cottage" and "Wapanak", 1960's. (Courtesy, Ike Wolgin)

"Belle View", facing Bolton Bay, was constructed along the shoreline where today's indoor swimming pool is located. William B. Bement, of Philadelphia, owned the Philadelphia Locomotive Works. His "Belle View" sported a six-story tower, attached to the home, which afforded excellent lake views in all directions.

William Bement sold Belle View to his friend, Colonel T. E. Roessle of Albany, who owned the Fort William Henry Hotel in Caldwell (Lake George Village). The Colonel sold the property to Frank McNamee, a stock broker from Albany, who passed it on to William Stoutenberg, a stock broker from New York City. Eventually, Belle View was sold to the Sagamore. It was torn down to accommodate the swimming pool and to improve the views from the hotel.

"Belle View"
The Sagamore,
Lake George, 1895.
M. O. Brown.
(Courtesy, Bolton
Historical Museum)

"Belle View" means *Beautiful View.* (Courtesy, Bolton Historical Museum)

"Villa Nirvana" belonged to John Boulton Simpson of New York City. He and his wife, Fanny, had rejected the Simpsons' family pawn brokerage business, so his father purchased for him the American Agency of the Estey Piano Company. Villa Nirvana became more than just their summer cottage; they began dividing their time equally between Bolton Landing and New York City. While at Bolton, J. B. Simpson became actively involved in the Episcopal Church and the Lake George (Yacht) Club, and he became a board member of both. He helped the church to acquire many of the fineries which still adorn the interior today, and was deeply involved in the organization of the Yacht Club throughout 1909 and

afterwards. The Simpson family's wealth was unfortunately balanced by family tragedy. Their baby son, Roy, died before reaching the age of three and is buried in Bolton's Huddle Cemetery. Their older son, John Boulton Jr., died at age fourteen. However, they had two daughters; In 1881, Francis Proddow Simpson was born, followed by sister Helen in 1890. Helen's birth was reported as being the, "first white child born on Green Island".

John Boulton Simpson
(Courtesy, Hugh Allen Wilson)

In 1877, the Simpsons began vacationing in Bolton. They enjoyed their summers while staying at the Mohican House Hotel. During the next five years they became close friends with fellow guests Warren, Burnham, Bement and Glendenning. These five millionaires would soon form a partnership to build the first Sagamore Hotel.

The Simpsons and other wealthy "Cottagers" along "Millionaires Row" arrived at Caldwell (Lake George Village) in private railroad coaches. Their personal steam yachts would meet them there and transport them to their summer mansions along the lake.

Simpson family's "Private Car" arriving at Caldwell (Lake George Village). (Courtesy, Hugh Allen Wilson)

John Boulton Simpson owned several boats over the years, but his showboat was his steam yacht "Fanita". It was eighty feet long, eleven feet across the beam and was capable of speeds of up to sixteen miles an hour. The yacht was always ready to be used for regattas and entertaining. Today, the Bolton Historical Museum on Main Street in Bolton Landing has an extensive exhibit on the Fanita, Villa Nirvana and the Simpsons. On display are the Fanita's wheel, clock, trophies, deck chair and other Simpson memorabilia and photographs.

Steam yacht *"Fanita"* at a
Sagamore Regatta.
(Courtesy, Hugh Allen Wilson)

"Villa Nirvana" was a showplace. Every corner of the cottage and property was impeccably maintained. The Lake George Mirror on August 12, 1893 stated that landscaper Ranny Wilson, "knows the botanical names of every plant in the Commodore's conservatories on the grounds surrounding this summer mansion. One valuable plant, the Night Blooming Cerius, has blossomed thirty or forty times this season."

"Villa Nirvana"
(Author's Collection)

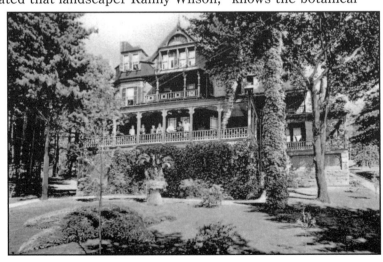

On August 13, 1898, The Mirror stated that Ranny's, "flower beds around Nirvana Cottage are gems of beauty. Mr. Wilson takes as much pride in keeping the grounds in order around Commodore Simpson's cottage as a debutante would in her coming out finery". Every tree was groomed and many shrubs were shaped to resemble a leaf, starfish, tortoise and butterfly. A flower garden spelled the words "Villa Nirvana" in peonies.

"Villa Nirvana" —
Nirvana means *Ultimate Union with God*.
(Courtesy, Hugh Allen Wilson)

V
I
L
L
A

N
I
R
V
A
N
A

(Courtesy, Hugh Allen Wilson)

Fanny and Helen Simpson at the
playhouse which still stands today.
(See page 118)
(Courtesy, Hugh Allen Wilson)

Green Island resident Jane
Gabriels once asked Helen
Simpson to briefly describe
herself. Helen said proudly —
"I'm a lady of the lake".

The Simpson family and
friends in John Boulton
Simpson's six cylinder
60hp Great Arrow Car at
the Sagamore Hotel, Lake
George, New York. Miss
Helen Simpson steering.
(Courtesy, Hugh Allen Wilson)

J. B. Simpson's private stable behind "Villa Nirvana".
(Courtesy, Bolton Historical Museum)

"Villa Nirvana" was more than a summer showplace — it was "Home" for many generations of the Simpson family during their extended summers at Bolton Landing. The home was filled with bustling activity, occasional tears and much laughter.

Nirvana has withstood the test of time for well over one hundred years, passing through the hands of only a few Sagamore families during its entire first century, most notably the Simpson's, future manager Karl P. Abbott and later hotel owner Louis Brandt.

Early "Nirvana"
(Courtesy, Hugh Allen Wilson)

"Nirvana" Today
(Photo by Author)

Each of the cottage properties had deed restrictions which were intended to protect the hotel's future. Cottage owners and guests were required to take all meals at the hotel and to purchase all of their ice, water and electricity there. New construction needed approval from the Green Island Improvement Company, and each cottage owner was required to maintain a "promenade walk" along the shoreline which was to be accessible for public use.

The First Sagamore Hotel
(1882 -1893)

After the first bridge was completed in the spring 1882, plans for construction on the new hotel moved forward rapidly. The stockholders hired John Jalet of Ticonderoga to oversee construction using blueprints drawn up by the Wilson Brothers, Civil Engineers and Architects from Philadelphia. Its design was of the Queen Anne shingled style and incorporated a visually "appealing combination of architectural styles resulting in varied levels and unexpected balconies", according to an early Lake George Mirror. In 1891, the Mirror stated that, "The house (hotel) is built so that guests can step out of almost any story to velvet lawns".

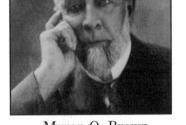

Myron O. Brown, formerly of the Mohican House, personally helped to supervise construction. He was its first manager, and he remained in that position until 1905. He, and the five investors, must have labored extensively to select the appropriate name for their new hotel. James Fenimore Cooper in his historical regional novel, "Last of the Mohicans", referred to Chingachgook as "The Great Sagamore" (or respected chief) of the Mohican Indians. This new hotel would be named, — *The Sagamore.*

Myron O. Brown
(Courtesy, Bolton Historical Museum)

Sagamore I - Architectural Drawing
The Sagamore, Green Island, Lake George, M.O. Brown, 1893. (Author's Collection)

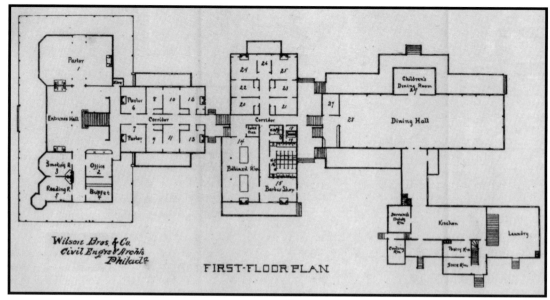

FIRST·FLOOR·PLAN

Wilson Bros. & Co.
Civil Engrs & Archts
Philada

Sloop Island

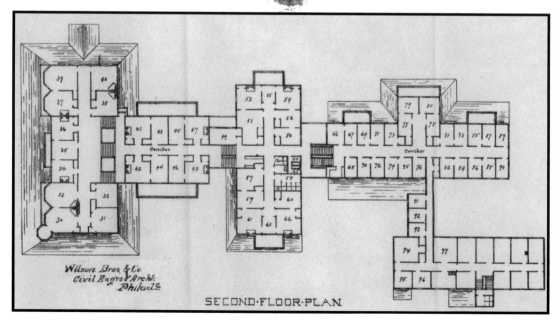

SECOND·FLOOR·PLAN

Wilson Bros. & Co.
Civil Engrs & Archts
Philada

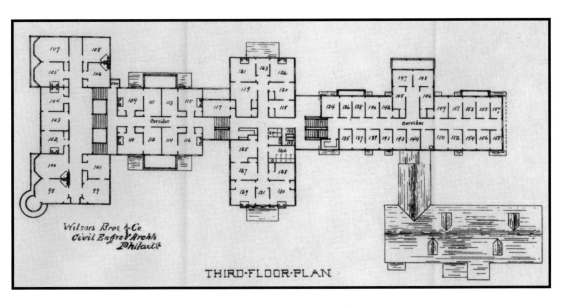

THIRD·FLOOR·PLAN

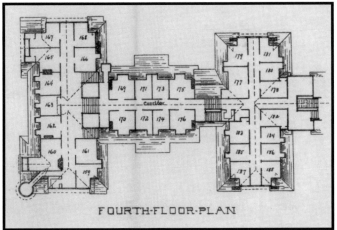

FOURTH·FLOOR·PLAN

THE·SAGAMORE
GREEN·ISLAND
LAKE·GEORGE
N·Y

(Author's Collection)

Drawing by S. R. Stoddard.   (Courtesy, Gordon Garlick)

Sagamore I Construction (1882 - 1883)

Construction on Sagamore I began in 1882 and continued throughtout the snowy winter and spring of 1883. Local carpenters and suppliers found plenty of opportunities for work and advancement on the various hotel projects.

The three and a half story hotel was an elongated H-shape with its southern end located at a high point forty feet above the lake.

Building of First Sagamore Hotel

It was designed in the shingled mode of the Queen Anne style, with some rooms sharing balconies while others were arranged in a more private nature.

1883

Four construction photos of Sagamore I.
(Courtesy, Bolton Historical Museum)

To have the docks completed quickly and on time was as important as having the bridge and hotel completed on time for the summer of 1883 because most of the new guests would be arriving by steamboat.

Constructing the docks for Sagamore I, Spring 1883.
(Courtesy, Gordon Garlick)

Sagamore Docks in Winter, by L. E. Taylor.
(Courtesy, Henry Caldwell)

First Bridge, and Sagamore I, in Winter.
(Courtesy, Bolton Historical Museum)

Rough road leading to stables on left, and Sagamore I, by S.R. Stoddard.
(Courtesy, Bolton Historical Museum)

The first large structure encountered after crossing the wooden bridge was the barn where the Sagamore's horses and carriages were housed. This building, although modified, still stands today on Green Island. (See page 118)

The Sagamore's Barn and Stables, 1883. Photo by Conkey.
(Courtesy, Bolton Historical Museum)

Barn and Stables, 1883, (Still standing, see page 118). In foreground, fresh grading for new golf course. Photo by Conkey. (Courtesy, Bolton Historical Museum)

Barn and Carriages. (Courtesy, Bolton Historical Museum)

Every early photographer and writer featured the beautiful grove of White Birch Trees surrounding the hotel. Photo by Conkey.
(Courtesy, Bolton Historical Museum)

"Tally-Ho" Stage and E. Burgess Warren's "Fisherman's Cottage" (where F. R. Smith's Marina stands today on Sagamore Road.)
(Courtesy, Hugh Allen Wilson)

The Sagamore's "Tally-Ho" Stage driven by coachman Harrington. Notice bridge and Green Island Golf Course in background. (Courtesy, Hugh Allen Wilson)

The first Sagamore opened to the public on July 2, 1883. The hotel's opening was highly anticipated and an immediate success. Many have written about the Sagamore's first year, however, I can think of no one better suited for writing its description than Seneca Ray Stoddard, Glens Falls photographer and author:

"The Sagamore has come. Long watched for; fondly hoped for; often promised, it has at last leaped, almost in a night, in a winter at least, strong and stately, full grown and as nearly as perfect as it well can be, before its expectant audience, impressing all with its majestic bearing and proportions. The Sagamore is not a savage, although representing in its title the proudest chieftain of a vanished tribe and like its distinguished prototype standing a head and shoulders above its fellows, but the new hotel on Green Island, at a point for years looked upon as the hotel site par excellence of this section, now utilized through the energy of Philidelphia capitalists and one of Lake George's most popular landlords, together forming a company possessed not only of a knowledge of what the best people have at home and naturally desire at a hotel, but also the skill and experience necessary to successfully manage the innumerable details in the

VIEW OF THE SAGAMORE AND ITS ENVIRONS.

| Its Situation, Villages, Hotels, and Summer Villas. | Lake George. | Its Islands, Walks, Drives, etc. |

The Sagamore, Lake George, 1889, M.O. Brown.
(Courtesy, Bolton Town Historian)

business of a great hotel.

The hotel building stands on high ground and commands, on every side, extended views of the lake and mountains. It is built in the style popularly supposed to belong to the sixteenth century; its varied porticoes, balconies and gables all admirably displayed by the harmonious colors with which it is painted. Within will be found every hotel convenience and comfort, including hydraulic passenger elevator, electric bells, telegraph office, etc. It is supplied with an abundance of pure running water, brought through pipes from a mountain on the mainland two miles distant. Many of the rooms are arranged en suite with outside entrances, and all rooms are illuminated with the Edison electric light. The interior finish is in the best of taste, the furniture being of native hard woods, polished.

Liberal provisions have also been made for outdoor amusements. The picturesque grounds, some seventy acres in extent, have been laid out in walks and drives encircling the entire island. Attractive lawn tennis and croquet grounds are here. The livery provisions are ample, the facilities for enjoying them complete in the beautiful drives along the west shore, north and south.

Sagamore I, 1883. Photo by Conkey.
(Author's Collection)

Aquatic amusements need not lanquish in want of means for enjoyment as a fleet of boats of various kinds will be found at the landing, ranging from the tiny skiff to the comfortable steam-yacht. From the ample dock, broad drives and walks lead through overhanging trees up to the south front of the hotel and along the west shore of the island to the handsome rustic bridge which connects it with the mainland.

The Horicon, Ticonderoga, and other steamers land at every regular trip during the season, making close connections with the railroad trains at Caldwell.

The Sagamore will accommodate 300 guests. Price of board $4.00 per day; $15.00 to $25.00 per week, according to room and length of stay. Special rates will be made for families. Address, M. O. Brown, Bolton Landing, N. Y.

My thoughts to-day
are far away.
And o'er Lake George
they freely stray;
My winged boat —
A bird afloat —
Swims 'neath
the purple
peaks remote.

The Sagamore, Lake George, 1895. M.O. Brown.
(Courtesy, Bolton Historical Museum)

Mr. Brown, the lessee, will be remembered as the proprietor of the Mohican House, and his popularity as such may be inferred from the fact that the patronage bestowed on that popular hostelry was limited only by its capacity." *Seneca Ray Stoddard*

Sagamore I, 1883. Photo by Jules A. Thatcher of Bolton Landing.
(Courtesy, Hugh Allen Wilson)

Veranda, Sagamore I. (Courtesy, Chapman Historical Museum)

The first Sagamore is easily distinguishable by the round cone-shaped turret on its tower and by its exterior siding, which featured white clapboards on the first two stories and dark shingles on the upper two stories.

West side of Sagamore I. (Courtesy, Bolton Town Historian)

East side, Sagamore I.
(Courtesy, Bolton Historical Museum)

Letterhead. (Courtesy, Henry Caldwell)

DISTANCE TABLE.—SAGAMORE TO						
NORTH.			SOUTH.			
Fourteen Mile Island,	0	2	Bolton,		0	1
Pearl Point,	1	3	Marion,		4	5
Hulett's,	7	10	Kattskill,		3	8
Sabbath Day Point,	2	12	Sheldon's		1	9
Silver Bay,	3	15	Cleverdale,		1	10
Hague,	3	18	Assembly Point,		1	11
Rogers Rock,	6	24	Caldwell,		3	14
Baldwin,	1	25				

WALKS AND DRIVES.—Distances in Miles.

Artist's Falls,	Walk, 1	Shelving Rock (top),	Row, 2, and climb
Indian Falls,	Row, 1¾, or walk, 2½	Black Mountain (top),	Row, 5, and climb
Barton's Ledge,	Row or walk 5.	Paradise Bay,	Row, 3
Pinnacle (top),	Walk, 2	Caldwell,	Drive, 10
Cat Mountain (top),	Walk, 3	Caldwell and Prospect Mountain (top),	Drive or boat and cable road
N. W. Bay, Creek and Falls,	Row, 5		
Huddle Bay and Falls,	Row, 1½	Bolton Pond,	Drive
Basin Bay,	Row, 2½	Edgecomb Pond,	Drive
Log Bay,	Row, 2	Schroon River,	Drive
Shelving Rock Falls,	Row, 2, and walk, ½	Federal Hill,	Drive
Calf Pen,	Row, 2½	Warrensburg,	Drive
Buck Mountain (top),	Row, 3, and climb	N. W. Bay,	Drive or boat

Early advertisement. *Sagamore, Green Island*, 1889. M.O. Brown.
(Courtesy, Bolton Town Historian)

The developers designed the hotel to fit comfortably into the wooded landscape of the island. Photo by S.R. Stoddard. (Courtesy, Bolton Town Historian)

From

Harper's

Monthly

" Just at dusk the steamer landed midway in the lake at Green Island, where the scenery is the boldest and most romantic ; from the landing a park-like lawn, planted with big trees, slopes up to a picturesque Hotel. Lights twinkled from many a cottage window and from boats in the bay, and strains of music saluted the travelers. It was an enchanting scene.

" The genius of Philadelphia again claims the gratitude of the tourist, for the Sagamore Hotel is one of the most delightful hostelries in the world. A peculiar, interesting building, rambling up the slope on different levels, so contrived that all the rooms are outside, and having a delightful irregularity, as if the house had been a growth. Naturally a hotel so dainty in its service and furniture, and so refined, was crowded to its utmost capacity. The artist could find nothing to complain of in the morning except that the incandescent electric light in his chamber went out suddenly at midnight and left him in blank darkness in the most exciting crisis of a novel. Green Island is perhaps a mile long. A bridge connects it with the mainland, and besides the hotel it has four picturesque stone and timber cottages. At the north end are the remains of the English entrenchments of 1775—signs of war and hate, which kindly nature has almost obliterated with sturdy trees. With the natural beauty of the island art has little interfered ; near the hotel is the most stately grove of white birches anywhere to be seen, and their silvery sheen, with occasional patches of sedge, and the tender sort of foliage that Corot liked to paint, gives an exceptional refinement to the landscape. One needs, indeed, to be toned up by the glimpses, under the trees, over the blue water, of the wooded craggy hills, with their shelf-like ledges, which are full of strength and character. The charm of the place is due to this combination of loveliness and granitic strength."

Article by Charles Dudley Warner, " Their Pilgrimage."

The Sagamore, Green Island, Lake George, 1893. M.O. Brown. (Author's Collection)

Interior Views of Sagamore I

Office and Hall. Photo by S.R. Stoddard.
(Courtesy, Bolton Historical Museum)

The Main Parlor. (Courtesy, Bolton Historical Museum)
Parlor Sketch, 1889. M.O. Brown. (Courtesy, Bolton Town Historian)

Myron O. Brown,
Proprietor.

Bolton Landing,
Lake George, N. Y.
June, 1889.

DINING ROOM, SAGAMORE HOTEL.

(Courtesy, Bolton Town Historian)

Dining Room, Sagamore I

*The Sagamore,
Green Island, Lake
George*, 1893. M.O.
Brown.
(Author's Collection)

Photo by S.R. Stoddard. (Courtesy, Bolton Historical Museum)

The Small Parlor. Photo by S.R. Stoddard. (Courtesy, Henry Caldwell)

The Ball Room. *The Sagamore, Green Island, Lake George,* 1889. M.O. Brown.
(Courtesy, Bolton Town Historian)

Green Island Golf Course

In 1889, a nine hole golf course opened on Green Island behind the hotel. The Lake George Mirror stated on June 9, 1915 that, "It is conceded by all hotel men these days that a golf course is a prime necessity. It spells the difference in many cases between a profitable and losing operation of the house, and it has a magic drawing power that seems to the uninitiated out of all proportion to the other attributes of a resort property. For many years, this lack was deplored at the Sagamore". The golf course was situated immediately after crossing the bridge onto Green Island so that players from other local hotels and clubs could access the golf course without interfering with the peaceful activities surrounding the hotel and its guests. It was also necessary to provide access to the course from the stable area because these itinerate sportsmen arrived by horse and carriage.

Sketches from, *The Sagamore on Lake George,* T.E. Krumbholz. (Courtesy, Ike Wolgin)

Green Island Nine Hole Golf Course, looking Northwest. Sawmill Bay in the background. Stables at left. *The Sagamore, Green Island,* 1889. M.O. Brown. (Courtesy, Bolton Town Historian)

Putting on the Eighth Green. *The Sagamore, Green Island,* 1889.
M.O. Brown. (Courtesy, Bolton Town Historian)

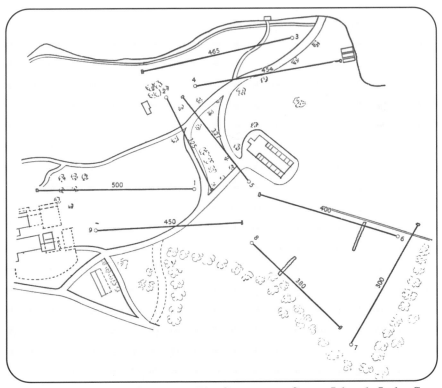

The Green Island Golf Course. *The Sagamore, Green Island, Lake George,*
M.O. Brown. (Courtesy, Gordon Garlick)

"The main hall and office, and the principal parlor and reading and smoking rooms are on the main floor, looking out upon a semi-circular lawn with flower-bordered walks leading down to the steamboat-landing, and revealing between its stately trees delightful vistas of lake and islands beyond."[1]

Lawn and Docks. Photo by Conkey. (Courtesy, Bolton Historical Museum)

NORTH.

LANDINGS.	Daily, except Sunday.	Daily, except Sunday.	Daily.	Daily, except Sunday.	Sundays only.
	A.M.	P.M.	P.M.	P.M.	A.M
Leave Caldwell	9.30	4.30	1.30	7.20	11.15
" Assembly Point	9.45	4.45	1.50	7.45	11.35
" Cleverdale	9.50	4.50	2.00	7.55	11.45
" Sheldon's	9.55	4.55	2.05	8.00	11.50
" Trout Pavilion	10.00	5.00	2.15	8.10	11.55
" Kattskill	10.05	5.05	2.20	8.15	12.00 M.
					P.M.
" Marion	10.20	5.20	2.40	8.30	12.15
" Bolton	10.35	5.35	2.50	8.45	12.30
" Sagamore	10.40	5.40	2.55	8.50	12.35
" 14-Mile Island	10.50	5.50	3.05	9.00	12.45
" Hundred Islands	10.55	5.55	3.10	9.05	12.50
" Pearl Point	11.00	6.00	3.15	9.10	12.55
" Paradise Bay	....	....	3.25	....	....
" Hulett's	11.35	6.40	....	....	1.30
" Sabbath Day Point	11.45	6.50	....	....	1.40
" Silver Bay	11.55	7.00	....	....	1.50
	P.M.				
" Hague	12.10	7.25	....	....	2.10
" Rogers Rock	12.30	7.45	....	....	2.30
Arrive Baldwin	12.50	7.50	....	....	....

SOUTH.

LANDINGS.	Daily, except Sunday.	Daily, except Sunday.	Daily.	Daily, except Sunday.	Sundays only.
	P.M.	A.M.			
Leave Baldwin	1.00	7.20	...	....	....
				P.M.	
" Rogers Rock	1.05	7.25	....	4.15	....
" Hague	1.35	7.40	....	4.35	....
" Silver Bay	1.45	8.00	....	4.55	....
" Sabbath Day Point	2.00	8.15	....	5.05	....
" Hulett's	2.10	8.20	....	5.15	....
			P.M.		
" Paradise Bay	....	3.25	....		A.M.
" Pearl Point	2.50	8.55	3.35	5.45	6.45
" Hundred Islands	2.55	9.00	3.40	5.50	6.50
" 14-Mile Island	3.00	9.05	3.45	5.55	6.55
" Sagamore	3.10	9.10	3.55	6.05	7.05
" Bolton	3.15	9.15	4.05	6.10	7.10
" Marion	3.30	9.30	4.25	6.30	7.25
" Kattskill	3.45	9.45	4.40	6.45	7.40
" Trout Pavilion	3.50	9.50	4.45	6.50	7.45
" Sheldon's	3.55	9.55	4.50	6.55	7.50
" Cleverdale	4.00	10.00	5.00	7.00	7.55
" Assembly Point	4.10	10.10	5.10	7.10	8.05
Arrive Caldwell	4.25	10.35	5.40	7.25	8.45

NEW YORK TO MONTREAL.

STATIONS.	ROUTE.	Daily, except Sunday.	Daily, except Sunday.
		A.M.	A.M.
Leave NEW YORK	N. Y. C. & H. R. R. R.	9.30	12.10
			P.M.
" "	Night Boats.	....	6.00
			A.M.
" "	Day Boats.		8.40
		P.M.	
" Albany	D. & H. R. R	1.00	6.50
" Troy	"	1.50	6.50
" Saratoga	"	3.00	8.10
" Fort Edward	"	3.25	8.40
" CALDWELL	Lake George Steamers.	4.30	9.30
" Sagamore	"	5.40	10.40
			P.M.
Arrive BALDWIN	"	7.50	12.50
Leave FORT TICONDEROGA	Lake Champlain Steamers.	....	1.30
		A.M.	
" Westport	"	7.00	3.20
" Burlington	"	9.20	5.20
" Bluff Point (Hotel Champlain), Landing for Catholic Summer School	"	10.30	6.35
Arrive Plattsburgh	"	10.50	7.00
		P.M.	
" MONTREAL	G. T. Railway.	3.00	9.50

MONTREAL TO NEW YORK.

STATIONS.	ROUTE.	Daily, except Sunday.	Daily, except Sunday.
		A.M.	P.M.
Leave MONTREAL	G. T. Railway.	10.00	7.00
		P.M.	A.M.
" Plattsburgh	Lake Champlain Steamers.	2.45	7.00
" Bluff Point (Hotel Champlain), Landing for Catholic Summer School	"		2.55	7.10
" Burlington	"	5.20	8.40
" Westport	"	7.20	10.10
			P.M.
Arrive FORT TICONDEROGA	"	....	12.25
" BALDWIN	D. & H. R. R.	....	12.50
		A.M.	
" Sagamore	Lake George Steamers.	9.10	3.10
" Caldwell	"	10.35	4.25
		P.M.	
" Saratoga	D & H. R. R.	12.05	6.12
" Troy	"	1.50	7.30
" Albany	"	1.15	7.50
		A.M.	
" NEW YORK	N. Y. C. & H. R. R. R.	5.00	6.30
" "	West Shore R. R.	8.00	7.50
" "	Night Boats.	....	6.00
			P.M.
" "	Day Boats.	....	5.30

Boat and Train Schedules. *Sagamore, Green Island,* 1889. M.O. Brown.
(Courtesy, Bolton Town Historian)

The Docks

Swim Dock. Photo by S.R. Stoddard.
(Courtesy, Ike Wolgin)

Sketch. *Sagamore, Lake George,*
1889. M.O. Brown.
(Courtesy, Bolton Town Historian)

Docks and Guideboats. (Courtesy, Bolton Historical Museum)

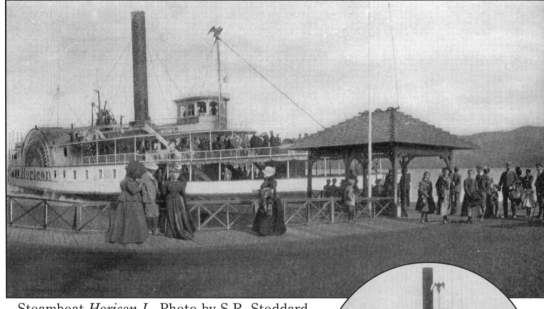

Steamboat *Horicon I.* Photo by S.R. Stoddard.
(Author's Collection)

The arrivals of the steamboats were highly
anticipated daily events. New guests arrived,
former guests departed and hotel personnel
scurried about in frenzied preparation.

Horicon I. Photo by J.S. Wooley. (Author's Collection)

Dock and Steamboat *Ganouski*.
Photo by S.R. Stoddard. (Author's Collection)

Mohican I approaching Sagamore Dock. Photo by J.S. Wooley. (Author's Collection)

Sagamore I – Burns June 27, 1893

After ten highly successful summer seasons, tragedy struck the Sagamore Hotel. Newspapers throughout the country carried the same headline — "The Sagamore in Flames". The Lake George Mirror carried the story in detail for the Lake George region on July 1, as follows: "The beautiful Sagamore is no more. A romance in wood; in the twinkling of an eye it was outlined in fire, and the nonce became a romance in crimson flame. The ruin is complete. It is hard to believe that this lovely summer palace is now only smouldering heaps of ashes. The main building, parlors and offices, its hundreds of feet of piazzas, the second building with its private offices and reading rooms, "Yea ancient Sagamore seated in his golden canoe," the great dining hall, music hall, engine room and kitchens all devoured by the red and ruddy flames.

I reached the Kenesaw (Hotel) at Fourteen Mile island about half-past eight o'clock Tuesday morning and while leaning against the pilot house of the Ticonderoga, caught the eye of Hannibal Allen, who shouted "It's too bad the Sagamore is burned, is it not?" I asked West Finkel, Mr. Allen is given to star-tling jokes when all at once three or four distinct, though small, columns of smoke streaming heavenwards caught my eye above the tall trees on Sagamore island. The pilot handed me a glass and the truth burst startlingly upon us. The fanciful and elegantly built summer hotel had disappeared in a night.

The feeling was one of angry surprise that the devouring elements had dared to approach and destroy that beautiful fabric. When the Ticonderoga had reached the Sagamore pier, the view was anything but picturesque. The broad lawns were strewn with furniture, piled in indiscriminate confusion where it must have been dropped by the hurrying crowd of waiters and employees. Cushions, mattresses, pillows, stands, tables, chairs, clocks, boxes and trunks. There was a line like the plan of an outlying breastwork thrown up around the outer circle of the fire. The tall chimneys, burdened with handsome terra-cotta and marble fireplaces, stood proudly erect as if defying the smouldering ruin. The lawns close to the hotel were scorched and blackened, flower beds trampled upon and the great forest trees that stood nearest the tower and which from their lofty heights looked down on the Sagamore and his canoe, were blackened and burned and foliage wilted and shriveled by the intense heat.

The eye turned every way but toward the ruins. The picture of the former beautiful summer palace was yet too plain to be rudely dispelled by looking at the vulgar masses of bricks and mortar and piles of ashes. Involuntarily the glance roved in the direction of the famous (four) cottages. On the left the cottage of General Banks (Bement's) and a few rods to the north that of Commodore J.B. Simpson, showed that much of the goods saved had been taken there for safe keeping. On the right, to the east of the hotel, the cottage of Mr. E. Burgess Warren and Mr. George Burnham were intact. The stables, some distance from the house, and the bowling alley and one or two other small buildings are left standing. The ruin and desolation was complete.

In a quiet chat with Mr. M.O. Brown, the proprietor, I heard all that could be learned of the origin of the fire and the terrors of the night. "I was awakened," said he, "by the cry of fire given by the watchman as he ran through the building. The room was aglow. The flames had already burst from the interior of the laundry building and were moving fast toward the main structure. The watchman says that he saw the fire in the drying room and hastened to the door, thinking he could put it out with the hose and hydrant in that part of the building. The minute he opened the door, the sudden draft enabled the flames to gain headway and before he could obtain a glance into the interior, the flames and smoke swept out into the hall and drove him from his place. He saw the imminent danger that the house was in and gave the alarm. Waiters and employees came tumbling from their beds and down the fire escapes by the score. The guests took more time and began packing their clothing at once.

An effort was made to get two streams on the fire from the hydrant near the main building, but the fierceness of the fire soon drove the pipemen to the rear. The flames spread to the dining room and music hall and the matter of the destruction of the hotel was only a question of time. In an instant, so it seemed, the great dining hall was a mass of red hot fire. The employees did everything that could be done to save the property of the guests. Some of the girls employed in the house lost most of their clothing and there were many narrow escapes.

One matter of congratulation was that no one was injured. At the time of the fire there were 150 asleep in the hotel — employees and guests. Ample time was given so that all were enabled to make their escape and watch from a safe distance the destruction of the house. Stories were abroad Tuesday that the water supply was inefficient. I was informed by creditable witnesses that there was force enough to burst three lines of hose, but that the fire spread so quickly that it was impossible to save anything.

One of the guests gave me an idea of the grandness of the sight from the lawn when the front of the structure burst into flames. The golden Indian on the tower stood it as long as he could and then evidently concluding that this was by all odds the hottest fire he had ever experienced, collapsed and shot away in his light canoe, bound for the happy hunting grounds. The flames wreathed the balconies and piazzas and pillars with glittering gems of fiery lace work. The windows were illuminated, then the fire showed through the boards, intertwining and spreading and twisting in a thousand glowing scintillations.

The light of the conflagration could be seen for miles. It was seen from Baldwin (near the Town of Ticonderoga) by the watchman of the steamer but owing to the intervening mountains, he had no way of properly locating the fire. The flames were seen from the head of the lake on Assembly Point, Kattskill Bay and other points and most everybody was prepared to hear in the morning that the Sagamore had been destroyed.

The Sagamore was built in the winter and spring in 1883 and opened in July of that same year. There were 250 guest rooms and the house was capable of accommodating 400 guests. The loss on house and furniture as closely estimated is roughly placed at $200,000.

It is too early to speculate on the prospects of rebuilding the hotel, though from all appearances the site is much too valuable to be allowed to go to waste. The grounds are in complete order and it cost considerable money to build the docks, stables, bridges, waterworks and other necessary features of the hotel. Mr. William B. Bement, the principal stockholder, arrived on the steamer Horicon Tuesday forenoon direct from New York or Philadelphia.

Commodore Simpson left for New York City Monday. Mrs. Simpson telegraphed him Tuesday morning and it is expected that he will return at once.

Mr. Warren could not say what the prospects were for rebuilding. It was altogether too early in the day. The matter would be settled at a meeting of the directors which no doubt would be called soon.

The amount of insurance, as near as could be learned, is about $128,000. In a short interview with General Robert Lenox Banks at his cottage on the Sagamore grounds, the General said that he was undecided what to do, that the cottagers would undoubtedly hold a conference, and if the matter could be arranged, they would remain on the grounds.

Among the Sagamore guests who were at the hotel at the time of the fire were Mr. and Mrs. J.S. Frothingham, of New York City. The lady and gentleman saved all their trunks and are now stopping at the Mohican House, Bolton-On-Lake George.

The loss of the Sagamore is a blow to the whole lake."

Desk Bell from Sagamore I

Of the few objects salvaged from the ruins after the great fire, perhaps the most interesting discovery was that the Main Desk Bell was only slightly scorched and otherwise left intact and in good working order. This bell is currently on display at the Bolton Historical Museum along with many other early Sagamore photographs and memorabilia. (Photo, Author's Collection)

Sagamore I Fire

Burned June 27, 1893. (Courtesy, Bolton Historical Museum)

Chimneys, with fireplaces showing floor levels. (Courtesy, Gordon Garlick)

Sagamore I Fire. (Courtesy, Hugh Allen Wilson)

Guidebook author Seneca Ray Stoddard had already published his 1893 guidebook, thus he was forced to place this stamp over each Sagamore Hotel page.
(Courtesy, Henry Caldwell)

1 Dome Island; 2 Elizabeth Island; 3 Kattskill Bay; 4 Lo
French Mountain; 6 Recluse Island; 7 Canoe Island; 8 Be
9 Caldwell (not visible).

THE SAGAMORE (on Green Island,
miles), M. O. Brown, manager. Price o
$3.50 to $4.00 per day. .50 to $25.00 p
according to room and season. Open Ju
October. The steamers land on ever
trip through the lake connecting with the

BURNED JUNE 27, 1893.

1893, No Sagamore on Green Island. (Courtesy, Bolton Town Historian)

The Second Sagamore Hotel
(1893-1914)

With Sagamore I burned and closed, there was no Sagamore summer business season during 1893, however, the "Cottage" owners' homes were spared, and their families needed a dining hall. To solve this problem, the bowling alley building, which was also spared from burning, was converted into a temporary dining room. Its furnishings had been rescued during the fire.

Bowling Alley as temporary dining room, 1893. (Courtesy, Bolton Historical Museum)

The Design for the new Sagamore II. (Author's Collection)

Once again, the Wilson Brothers of Philadelphia were called in to design the new hotel. There were two noticeable changes. The turret on the tower no longer had a conical roof — it was octagonal, and the siding was all clapboard — not shingled on the upper half. John Jalet of Ticonderoga would once again oversee the project. Before construction could begin, the site had to be totally prepared and the old chimneys taken down. To cut costs, the new hotel would be constructed upon the same foundation as Sagamore I. Lumber for the construction was to be hauled in by many teams of oxen, driven by local farmers. On Monday August 2nd, carpenters began laying the stacks of timber, and on Tuesday August 3rd, the framing commenced with a workforce of ninety men. The Lake George Mirror stated on September 9, 1893 that, "work will be pushed forward as rapidly as possible," and on December 14th, it said that, "work on the new Sagamore was suspended on Saturday to be resumed when it is easier to keep warm." As work moved on and off throughout the winter between cold spells, the March 9, 1894 Mirror explained, "work on the Sagamore Hotel resumed Monday with about thirty men." Bolton Landing photographer Jules A. Thatcher was hired by the owners to photograph the entire construction of the hotel.

Workmen and Oxen Team. (Courtesy, Bolton Historical Museum)

Apparently, there was some difficulty about settling the insurance claim from Sagamore I which delayed the framing of Sagamore II until August of 1893. This new hotel was four feet higher from the ground than the first hotel, its drying house, engine room and boiler were detached, and the dance hall was separated from the main hotel structure.

Framing Sagamore II, August 3, 1893. (Courtesy, Ike Wolgin)

The Framers. Photo by J.A. Thatcher. (Courtesy, Bolton Town Historian)

September 26, 1893. Photo by J.A. Thatcher.
(Courtesy, Bolton Historical Museum)

Finished Sagamore II and Workmen. Photo by J.A. Thatcher.
(Courtesy, Henry Caldwell)

The new Sagamore II Hotel opened for business on June 26th, 1894. "Its picturesque style was that popularly supposed to belong to the sixteenth century, — rising, one back of another, with short flights of steps between, connected by open corridors with charming outlooks; its varied porticoes, balconies and gables admirably displayed in colors that harmonized richly with their native surroundings."[1] The fire had destroyed many trees, however, stands of birch, hemlocks and pines survived, and new trees were planted in strategic locations on the grounds. This new hotel offered, "electric lights, steam elevators, private bathrooms, billiard rooms, a bowling alley, reading rooms and ladies parlors, and, in short, every known modern convenience for the comfort and pleasure of guests. No expense was spared to make the New Sagamore the Finest Summer Resort Hotel in the World. — MYRON O. BROWN, Lessee and Proprietor, Bolton Landing, P.O. Warren Co., N.Y." Myron Brown remained on as host of Sagamore II until 1905. According to Seneca Ray Stoddard, the price of lodging was, — "$4.00 per day; $17.50 to $25.00 per week, according to time and season." The hotel received a fresh supply of spring water which was pumped from Edgecomb Pond on Federal Hill, about two miles away, five hundred feet above the lake.

Sagamore II Completed for Grand Opening on June 26, 1894. Photo by Thatcher.
(Courtesy, Bolton Historical Museum)

South View of Sagamore II. (Courtesy, Chapman Historical Museum)

Fishing Sketch. *The Sagamore on Lake George,* 1895. M.O. Brown. (Courtesy, Bolton Historical Museum)

East View of Sagamore II. (Author's Collection)

Sagamore II Office. *Sagamore, Green Island.* 1889. M.O. Brown.
(Courtesy, Bolton Town Historian)

Myron Brown said that, "Electricity plays an important part in this hostelry. Electric annunciators connect the office with the various rooms, the Edison incandescent electric light is used throughout the establishment, and special wires of the Western Union Telegraph and Telephone systems place the hotel in direct communication with the outside world."

Office and Stairs. Photo by J.A. Thatcher. (Courtesy, Ike Wolgin)

The hotel's, "interior finish is plain, but rich and substantial, showing massive beams, fireplaces of artistic designs in terra-cotta, tinted walls and joiner work in native woods." *Myron O. Brown*

The Reading Room. *Sagamore, Lake George,* 1895. M.O. Brown.
(Courtesy, Bolton Historical Museum)

The Parlor. *Sagamore, Lake George,* 1895. M.O. Brown.
(Courtesy, Bolton Historical Museum)

Dining Room. *Sagamore, Lake George,* 1895. M.O. Brown. (Courtesy, Bolton Historical Museum)

This original dinner menu for September 4, 1897, is on display at the Bolton Historical Museum.

The Sagamore Lake George, N.Y.
DINNER

Soup

CREAM OF CHICKEN   *Amontillado*

Hors d' Oeuvres

OLIVES   PICKLES   RADISHES

Fish

TUBAN OF LAKE GEORGE BASS, REGENCE   *Rudesheimer*

PARISIENNE POTATOES

Relieve

TIMBALE OF CHICKEN, ROUCHILE   *Sauterne*

Entrees

SWEETBREAD BRESE AU PETIS POIS   *Pommery Sec*

FILLET OF BEEF AU MUSHROOMS   STRING BEANS

PUNCH A LA ROMAINE

Roast

SQUAB SUR CANOPE   *Pontet Canet*

CELERY, MAYONAISE

VANILLA ICE CREAM

FRUIT   CAKE   CAFE NOIR

CORDIAL

Advisory Board   *The Sagamore,*
Traders Fire Lloyds.   *September 4, 1897.*

Generating Plant — Electricity was required for lighting, annunciators, telegraph and telephones. The generating plant behind the hotel consumed a generous supply of firewood. Photo by Thatcher, 1908. (Courtesy, Bolton Historical Museum)

Greenhouse — A staff of gardeners was employed to keep the grounds properly groomed. The greenhouse housed young flowers and shrubs, and started young vegetables for the garden to assist in supplying food for the hotel. Photo by Thatcher. (Author's Collection)

Wooden Bridge, 1895. (Courtesy, Bolton Historical Museum)

By 1896, the original wooden bridge (above) needed replacing. The hotel stockholders decided to replace it with an iron bridge which would leave the center span open for boat travel. The center photo shows the bridge from the south, and the bottom photo views the bridge from the north.

New Iron Bridge, May 7, 1896. (Both photos, Courtesy, Gordon Garlick)

Maintenance Crew and
Hunting Party.
(Courtesy, Bolton Historical
Museum)

The Front Piazza. (Courtesy, Bolton Town Historian)

"Tally-Ho Stage", Sagamore II. (Courtesy, Bolton Town Historian)

In August of 1899, the Lake George Mirror stated that, "Proprietor Hubble and Manager Curran, of the Sagamore livery, are conducting a first class establishment on Green Island for this great hotel. I looked over the carriage room recently and found that the new proprietor had purchased a first class line of three and two seater carriages. The horses here are stylish and driven by careful drivers, so there is no fear of an accident." A few years later, a "Revival of Coaching" was boasted. "The Lake George Stage & Transportation Company organized to run a regular line of four-horse Concord Coaches from the Sagamore to the railroad station at Caldwell (Lake George Village), carrying the United States Mail and Express matter. It has perfected all arrangements to convey passengers to and fro, meeting such trains as the steamboats do not; thus offering the choice of land or water transit, and reviving a feature of Lake George travel in bygone days when the old coaches carried their parties over this historic ground. They have leased the stables of the hotel for a term of years, and an entirely new and elegant outfit of wagons, carriages, and buck-boards are available. A feature is the Tally-Ho coach of English pattern and make, which may be chartered by the day or trip, and will be accompanied by an experienced driver as well as a guard."[1] In July of 1901, the Warrensburgh News said, "a horse belonging to the Sagamore livery died Sunday while returning from a trip to Caldwell. It was in a team and was in charge of a driver from the livery named Miller. The animal was taken sick near the Marion House and died in about twenty minutes. It had been driven carefully and the cause of its death is a mystery. The driver got a horse from the Marion House livery to bring his party home."

Sagamore II "Amusements"

"Sagamore March", 1896.
(Courtesy, Ike Wolgin)

The hotel offered, "billiards and bowling within, and croquet, tennis, polo, and archery without. Riding provided for in the extensive stables on the island. Fishing, rowing, sailing or steaming are all made attractive by respectable attendance, and a fleet of boats ranging from the tiny skiff to comfortable steam yachts (fare $1.50). A large hall for music and social gatherings has been built."[1] "Tennis, is perhaps, the most popular outdoor game. The courts at the Sagamore are ideal and are used by some of America's foremost players. The young people will take pride in having climbed some of the nearby mountains, which vary from 1000 to 2600 feet in height. As they are rather precipitous, it is strenuous work, but a good lunch and a wonderful panorama of the lake make the exertion well worthwhile."[2]

Sketches from *Sagamore, Lake George,* 1895. M.O. Brown and
The Sagamore on Lake George, T.E. Krumbholz.

Golf on Green Island, Sagamore II

In July of 1909, the Lake George Mirror wrote – "On its (Green Island's) diversified surface, room is found for golf links with very interesting hazards." In August of 1900, the Mirror reported, "A handicap tournament for mixed fours was held recently at the Sagamore. Twelve holes were played at medal play. The four lowest scores qualified for the semi-finals. The semi-finals and finals were twelve holes, match play. The entrance fee was one dollar for each couple. There were first and second prizes.

In 1899, M.O. Brown advertised the, "Ground Rules" for play at the Green Island Golf Course. It stated, "A ball lying on a green, other than the one being played, *must* be dropped back on the line of play. No penalty.–If a ball lie or be lost in water, another may be dropped. One stroke penalty. A ball out of bounds may be lifted and dropped. One stroke penalty.–On drives from tee, a ball may be lifted from a drain or a stone gutter and dropped back on line of play without penalty. On other strokes it may be lifted and dropped with one stroke penalty.–A ball may be lifted from and teed or dropped behind any other difficulty. Two strokes penalty if teed, one stroke if dropped.–A ball resting within a club's length of any tee within the fair green or of any building, may be dropped a club's length from said tee or building without penalty.–Roads (but not side paths) are "hazards".–A ball is "out of bounds" when resting within the garden to the right (west) of the fourth hole, the woods to the right (east and north) of the 2d and 3d holes.–A ball resting on the face or top of a bunker may be dropped back one club's length without penalty.–A two-ball game always has right of way, and a one-ball game never has. A foursome has right of way through a threesome.–Terms of Membership – is limited to regular guests of the hotel, cottagers and holders of cards of invitation (not transferable). Violation of any rule may result in peremptory cancelation of membership. Special hours for instruction and practice for ladies, children and men will from time to time be adopted and posted."

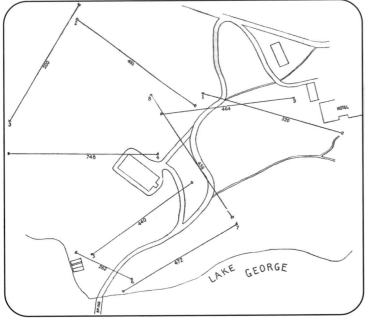

Golf Course, Sagamore II showing Fairway changes. *The Sagamore, Green Island, Lake George, NY,* 1899. M.O. Brown. (Courtesy, Bolton Town Historian)

New "Bow" Curved Porch, 1905. (Courtesy, Bolton Town Historian)

On June 17, 1905, the Lake George Mirror reported that Colonel Linsley, proprietor of the Hampton Terrace in North Augusta, Georgia, had leased the hotel and that, "Marvelous changes have been wrought on the property since last year at an expense of over $60,000, and it is expected that the amount will reach $80,000 before all improvements are completed. The most noticeable change is the new hotel front which forms an imposing "bow". Included are new rooms, entire new furnishings and new baths."

Oval Photo.
(Courtesy,
Ike Wolgin)

Sagamore II, Early 1900's. (Author's Collection)

The Docks, Sagamore II

"The Line Steamers land on every regular trip through the lake, connecting with the trains at each end, and run from Caldwell to the Sagamore dock on the arrival of the evening train from the south."[1] Myron O. Brown.

Steamboat *Sagamore* approaching the Sagamore Hotel from the Narrows.
(Courtesy, Ike Wolgin)

Passengers waiting for the steamboat on the Sagamore Dock.
Photo by S.R. Stoddard. (Author's Collection)

Panoramic View of the Sagamore Dock.
Photo by Seneca Ray Stoddard. (Author's Collection)

Arrival of Steamboat *Sagamore*. (Author's Collection)

(Courtesy, Ike Wolgin)

The Lake George Mirror in August of 1895 stated, "This is the height of the season on Green Island — the hotel is full, the grounds are constantly promenaded, and all is at its liveliest. Old friends come back. New ones come daily. Coming once, the visit is always repeated. Everyone is satisfied, and all wonder how with no apparent fuss everything in the cuisine and the housekeeping department can be so continuously satisfactory. A more modest and efficient proprietor (M.O. Brown) and wife cannot be found anywhere than at the Sagamore."

Automobiles delivered passengers to the Dock. (Courtesy, Hugh Allen Wilson)

Steamboat *Mohican I,* (1894-1908) at the Sagamore. (Courtesy, Library of Congress)

The Sagamore Regatta

Highly anticipated competitive Regattas were conducted at the Sagamore every August with events in canoeing, sailing, swimming and motor boating. John Boulton Simpson often was chairman of the event. The winners received cash and prizes. The Regatta was the crowning midsummer event of the season.

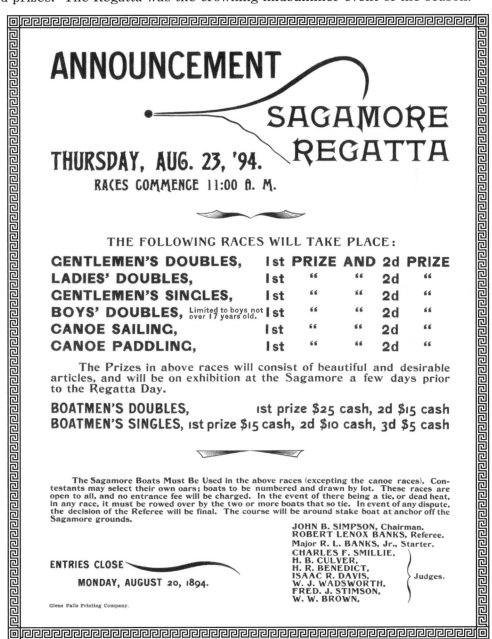

ANNOUNCEMENT

SAGAMORE REGATTA

THURSDAY, AUG. 23, '94.

RACES COMMENCE 11:00 A. M.

THE FOLLOWING RACES WILL TAKE PLACE:

GENTLEMEN'S DOUBLES,	1st PRIZE AND	2d PRIZE
LADIES' DOUBLES,	1st "	" 2d "
GENTLEMEN'S SINGLES,	1st "	" 2d "
BOYS' DOUBLES, Limited to boys not over 17 years old.	1st "	" 2d "
CANOE SAILING,	1st "	" 2d "
CANOE PADDLING,	1st "	" 2d "

The Prizes in above races will consist of beautiful and desirable articles, and will be on exhibition at the Sagamore a few days prior to the Regatta Day.

BOATMEN'S DOUBLES, 1st prize $25 cash, 2d $15 cash
BOATMEN'S SINGLES, 1st prize $15 cash, 2d $10 cash, 3d $5 cash

The Sagamore Boats Must Be Used in the above races (excepting the canoe races). Contestants may select their own oars; boats to be numbered and drawn by lot. These races are open to all, and no entrance fee will be charged. In the event of there being a tie, or dead heat, in any race, it must be rowed over by the two or more boats that so tie. In event of any dispute, the decision of the Referee will be final. The course will be around stake boat at anchor off the Sagamore grounds.

JOHN B. SIMPSON, Chairman.
ROBERT LENOX BANKS, Referee.
Major R. L. BANKS, Jr., Starter.
CHARLES F. SMILLIE,
H. B. CULVER,
H. R. BENEDICT,
ISAAC R. DAVIS, } Judges.
W. J. WADSWORTH,
FRED. J. STIMSON,
W. W. BROWN,

ENTRIES CLOSE

MONDAY, AUGUST 20, 1894.

Glens Falls Printing Company.

Regatta Poster, 1894. (Courtesy, Gordon Garlick)

An August 1895 Lake George Mirror said, "Added interest will be given to the annual regatta of the Sagamore on the 26th by the tub and swimming races. The latter will be started by the diving method, giving to each contestant a fair and even start with the others, and the distance to be swimmed will be about four hundred feet. If some of the cottagers noted for their swimming feats enter the contest, especially some of the smaller children, a most interesting spectacle would be witnessed. Commodore Simpson is doing all in his power to make this years regatta a phenomenal success, and has gone to New York this week to purchase the prizes, which, due to the liberality of Sagamore guests, will be finer and more expensive than ever before. The prizes will be on exhibition in a show case at the hotel. The hotel has the biggest crowd ever at this resort."

Regatta Swim Race. (Courtesy, Hugh Allen Wilson)

Regatta Rowboats. (Courtesy, Hugh Allen Wilson)

Racing Rowboats.
(Courtesy, Hugh Allen Wilson)

Insets. (Courtesy, Bolton Town
Historian and Ike Wolgin)

Fay & Bowen, 1 Cylinder Races, 9–12 mph. (Courtesy, Bolton Town Historian)

The Sagamore Farmhouse on a Hillside above Bolton Landing.

To supplement the fresh food supply at the hotel, the Sagamore operated a farm north of Bolton Landing in the Padanaram settlement. These two photographs show the simple farmhouse which burned in 1913.

(Courtesy, Bolton Historical Museum)

Members of the Utowana Fish and Game Club at the Sagamore.
(Author's Collection)

Sagamore II at the end of its final season in 1913.   (Courtesy, Bolton Town Historian)

Sagamore II – Burns April 12, 1914, Easter Sunday

Following Easter Sunday, April 12, 1914, the Glens Falls Star reported , –
**"Sagamore Hotel Totally Destroyed by Fire," – "Palatial Lake George
Hotel Burned Early Sunday Morning," – "Sagamore in Ashes."**

"The palatial Sagamore Hotel, at Bolton Landing, the largest and finest summer resort on Lake George, was completely destroyed by fire at an early hour
Sunday morning. The loss is estimated at $300,000 and the insurance was
$150,000. The origin of the fire is unknown, but from the fact that it started on
the outside and near the dining room on the southeast side of the building, incen-
diarism is strongly suspected.

The fire was discovered at 2:50 o'clock by J. Wilson Ward and in less than an
hour the magnificent hotel was but a mass of smouldering ruins. Mr. Ward
aroused the central telephone operator and she summoned to the scene as many
men as could be reached to form a bucket brigade. When the crowd arrived at
the burning structure on Green Island, a short distance from the village, the
flames had gained such headway that nothing could be done to check them.
Neither was it possible to gain entrance to the building, therefore none of its con-
tents could be saved. The furniture destroyed included furniture owned by persons who passed the summer in the hotel. The nearest outbuildings, the engine
and boiler house and the laundry, were saved with little effort as they were of
brick and steel construction. Of the six cottages now on the hotel grounds, only
two were at anytime threatened. These were owned by E. Burgess Warren and
the George Burnham estate, both of Philadelphia. The stables being a consider-
abe distance from the hotel were not endangered. Engineer, B.C. Green, was
working in the engine room Saturday but as far as could be learned, nobody was
in the hotel. The caretaker, Sheridan G. Finkle, was in Schenectady Saturday
night and expected to remain there over Sunday, but was called home on account
of the fire. He could offer no explanation as to the probable cause of the conflagration. The big building made a spectacular fire and threw a reflection upon the
sky which was plainly visible in Glens Falls.

The Sagamore was a three story wooden building with about 350 rooms. Last
fall it was painted at a cost of $1,000 and many improvements had been made dur-
ing the winter, including several fire escapes which were erected at a large
expense. About $1,500 was also expended for improvements on the dock.

The hotel was built twenty-one years ago to replace the old Sagamore which
was also destroyed by fire. It was owned by the Green Island Improvement
Company, of which John Boulton Simpson, is president and the heaviest stockholder. E. Burgess Warren and the estate of the late George Burnham, of

Philadelphia, are also stockholders. The house enjoyed a large patronage under the management of T. Edmund Krumbholz, who has been in charge of it since 1907. The buildings were situated on a beautiful point of land, surrounded by great pine trees, and each season attracted the attention of thousands of tourists going through the lake because of its magnificent appearance.

The residents of Bolton expressed the opinion that the Hotel Sagamore has passed out of existence for all time, however, Mr. Simpson visited Bolton Monday and stated that the hotel will be rebuilt and on a much more up-to-date scale. Work will be started on the new structure as soon as insurance adjusters, through the agency of Charles W. Cool, have finished their work."

Ruins of Sagamore II. (Courtesy, Bolton Historical Museum)

Hiram Seaman, an early Bolton resident, entered an account of the fire in his personal diary:

"April 12, 1914, Easter Sunday – Methodist (church) bell rang at 2:30 a.m. – Sagamore on fire – Allie (Allen Seaman), Willie (William Seaman), and I with Harry Ward were the first men at the fire – west wind – everything burned that could!"

(Courtesy, Theta Curri)

After the fire, the hotel's grounds were closed to the public.

Elsie Baldwin is Bolton Landing's oldest living citizen. Born on June 15, 1902, she was almost twelve years old the night the Sagamore II burned. She is still mentally sharp, and still very independently living in her own home in Bolton Landing. When I visited Elsie this spring of 2001, she proudly informed me she is looking forward to her 99th birthday. When I asked her if she remembered the Sagamore fire, Elsie said, — "Oh,yes! I had invited my friend, Freida Finkle, to sleep overnite at my house that night. We were sound asleep when a man knocked on our windows to tell us that the Sagamore was on fire. I wasn't very awake and I didn't know what to say, so I asked him, "What am I supposed to do about it?" We all went outside and the glow from the huge fire lit up the sky!

The next morning we went over to see it. It was totally gone, but there were still a lot of small fires burning. Bolton Landing didn't have any fire department back then. The men formed a small bucket brigade and were passing pails of water up to the fire. I remember that a lot of people needed to find a place to eat. It was a big deal back then."

She went on to say, "Mr. (J.B.) Simpson was a very nice man. My father, Henry Truax, was in charge of Mr. Simpson's crew on the "Fanita". Every Fourth of July, Mr. Simpson would take our family on the boat to see the fireworks at the Fort William Henry Hotel in Lake George. He did that after the fire, too."

Hamlet of Bolton Landing, 1914, showing the southern end of Green Island without Sagamore II. Photo by Francis Bayle. (Courtesy, Bob Bayle)

Gold Cup Speedboat Races, July 1914

The Sagamore Hotel was to be the focal point of activities during the 12th Annual Gold Cup Speedboat Races which were to be held that summer on Lake George to determine the "Championship of North America". In the previous summer of 1913, Bolton Landing's Count Casimir Mankowski, in his "Ankle Deep", won the Gold Cup Challenge at the Thousand Islands, bringing the races to his home waters — Lake George, on July 31, 1914. The hotel grounds were roped off and the island was closed to automobiles. Temporary grandstands were erected on the steamboat pier and along Green Island's shoreline. The Glens Falls Star reported that, "One of the largest crowds that ever attended such an event thronged the shores of Lake George while many spectators occupied small craft in a space roped off on the lake. The grandstand and boxes on the Sagamore grounds were taxed to their capacity. Weather conditions were ideal and when the race was started at 5:15 o'clock there was a fair sky and only a slight wind." Unfortunately for the local fans, "Ankle Deep" became damaged after a series of races and was unable to complete the competition which was finally won by "Baby Speed Demon II".

A portion of the grandstand, located on the Sagamore Hotel's steamboat pier, for watching the Gold Cup Speedboat Races, 1914. (Courtesy, Bolton Historical Museum)

"Ankle Deep", Gold Cup Races, 1914. (Author's Collection)

1914 Race: "Hawkeye", "Ankle Deep", "P.D.Q., V". (Author's Collection)

"Baby Speed Demon II", Winner of Gold Cup, 1914. (Author's Collection)

The Third Sagamore Hotel

(Present)

Throughout 1914 and 1915, there were countless rumors surrounding the fate of the Sagamore Hotel property and Green Island. Many rumors were hopefully based with such detail that they were actually printed frequently in the local newspapers. Every time John Boulton Simpson came to Bolton Landing and "Villa Nirvana", a new rumor would surface, undoubtedly because Mr. Simpson was hopeful himself. With the corporation uncertain about plans to rebuild, a newly constructed dormitory for hotel employees was converted into a dining area in 1914 to serve the summer cottagers and to provide accommodations for a small handful of summer guests. Without a hotel to manage, successful hotelier T. Edmund Krumbholz took a position, which was supposed to be for only one year, at the Buckwood Inn at Shawnee, Pennsylvania.

In 1915, the Lake George Mirror wrote, "The plans for the new hotel are of a most elaborate nature, and if ever carried into construction, will produce a splendid hostelry. However, all this is on paper, and it is the earnest hope of everyone that conditions may so change that the transition from paper to realism may be accomplished." The reality was that World War I severely slowed the prospects for reconstruction to the extreme that a "For Sale" sign was placed along the lakefront where it remained until the summer of 1918. On July 4, 1918 the Bolton Home Defense Reserves were mustered into "Service of State" in an impressive ceremony on Green Island. There was still no hotel on the horizon.

Following World War I, strong enthusiasm for major reconstruction was dampened, so a "scaled down" plan was adopted. The Mirror reported earlier that the Green Island Improvement Company was contemplating, "– a more complete development of the island's ideal cottage sites, with correspondingly less emphasis than formerly upon the hotel feature. It is proposed to erect upon part of the ground occupied by the former hotel, a clubhouse of three floors, the upper two to be devoted to bed-rooms with baths. On the ground floor will be the lounge, writing rooms, card rooms, etc., together with kitchen and dining-room facilities adequate for the accommodation of members and guests either in the clubhouse or in the cottages. At present, only a portion of the southern end of Green Island is occupied by cottages. Its entire length, three quarters of a mile, affords ideal cottage locations, all within easy distance of the proposed clubhouse. It is probable that the eastern side will be developed first."

In August of 1918, the "For Sale" sign along the shore was painted over. The new sign explained the new plan.

THIS IS THE FORMER SITE OF THE SAGAMORE HOTEL
AND WILL BE THE FUTURE HOME OF THE
SAGAMORE CLUB AND COTTAGE COLONY
A CLUB HOUSE AND COTTAGES ARE TO BE ERECTED HERE

(Courtesy, Bolton Historical Museum)

An elaborate plot-plan for many cottage sites surrounding the entire island was drawn up, however, this idea was eventually scaled down.

By 1920, construction on the smaller Sagamore "Club" was ready to begin. The Warrensburgh News for March 18, 1920 stated that, "In spite of the rough weather of the winter, the work of building the foundation for the new Sagamore hotel at Bolton Landing has been steadily pushed by contractor Joseph Fredella of Glens Falls, and is now about two-thirds completed. Contractor Fredella began his job last fall after the ground was frozen, and the work has progressed under the most difficult conditions with Sheridan Finkle of Bolton Landing as inspector of the work.

The ground where the hotel is to stand is a hardpan gravelly soil, frozen to a depth of from three to five feet. The soil has been removed by dynamite and wedging, by drilling and breaking off piece by piece to a depth of from five to seven feet and several hundred feet in width.

However, considering the continual cold weather, added to other inconveniences, the sand having to be hauled for nearly a mile through the deep snow, the foundation is about two-thirds finished. Plans called for solid concrete and stone laid in cement, ten and one-half feet high, basement floor full size of hotel, and the first of April will find the foundation finished, ready for the hotel to stand upon. The construction work will then begin."

But, construction did not begin, and plans continued to change. Two years later, a news article told, "Another movement is on foot to rebuild the Sagamore hotel at Bolton. It is proposed to organize a club to be operated on the plan of the Lake Placid Club. If this goes through, it is expected that work will be begun this fall on a central building in the modern club style. Ever since the Sagamore (II) burned, there has been talk of a new building and two years ago a foundation was built, but the cost was so great that the work was then stopped. Several cottages have been erected on Green Island since the hotel burned and a summer colony has been established." On January 3, 1918, J. B. Simpson purchased George Burnham's "East Cottage" from his heirs.

Back in 1901, the Bishop Ernest Milmore Stires family spent their summer vacation at the Sagamore Hotel. While there, their son was born, — the first boy ever born on the island and the second child ever to be born there. (The first, of course, was Helen Simpson). In 1903, the Sagamore agreed to build a handsome cottage for Reverend Stires on the west side for him to rent. This house, originally named "Airlea", became the birthplace of their fourth child. Thereafter, Reverend Stires purchased his own home which was located in Northwest Bay. In 1918, the Green Island Improvement Company sold his rental home on the island to Albert L. Judson, and in 1925, his widow Evelyn sold it to Mr. Peter D. Kiernan from Albany whose daughter Jane Gabriels still resides there with her family.

The Stires, Judson, Kiernan, Gabriels "Cottage" and early boathouse.
(Courtesy, Ike Wolgin)

Dr. Willy O. Meyer

In 1914, Dr. Willy O. Meyer from New York City, and his wife Lilly, built their summer cottage north of the Stires cottage. A remarkable aspect of this project was that the entire structure was completed in just sixty days. Dr. Meyer named his home "Ponemah" which in Mohican means "Indian Heaven". Dr. Meyer was a famous German born surgeon who once performed a secret operation on President Grover Cleveland's jaw. Willy Meyer received his medical degree from the University of Bonn in 1880. It was Meyer who brought to the attention of the surgical world the operative position called the Trendelenberg Posture. In 1884, he migrated to the United States, where he founded the New York Society and the American Society for Thoracic Surgery in 1917.

The home was later owned for many years by the O'Connor family, and for the last two decades at the end of the twentieth century, this first white home across the bridge has been owned by a family from the Albany - Schenectady area.

"Ponemah" today. (Photo by Author)

Dr. Willy Meyer's "Ponemah" as it once looked.
(Courtesy, Dorothy "Meyer" Craig)

Around 1920, Ernest Van Rensselaer Stires, the son of the Reverend Ernest M. Stires, became dissatisfied with the temporary facilities on Green Island. With the full support of John Boulton Simpson and financial support from stockholder William Girard Beckers, owner of the "Villa Marie Antoinette" estate in Huddle Bay, Mr. Stires took over the project of reconstructing the hotel. He rented the Burnham cottage and quickly became President of the Green Island Improvement Company.

The Warrensburgh News featured an article in 1922 which headlined, "TO REBUILD SAGAMORE —WORK WILL START AT ONCE — TO BE READY FOR 1923 SEASON." The article went on to say, "The reconstruction of the Sagamore hotel at Bolton will be started immediately. From good authority it has been learned that Monday, April 17, is the day the work is expected to be started. Ernest V. R. Stires, a New York builder, and his Uncle, J. E. R. Carpenter, an architect, have completed the arrangements and will be in charge of the work. About $300,000 will be expended this summer and early next year when it is expected that the hotel will be open to the public. It is planned to have most of the buildings and improvements completed by fall. It is proposed to spend about $25,000 to the sewerage system, water system and docks.

The Sagamore was one of the largest and best hotels on Lake George and its loss has had considerable effect upon the number of summer visitors to that section. The rebuilding of the famous hostelry will be a joy to the residents of this section and to the hundreds of visitors who chose that stop along Lake George for their summer vacations."

A later article adds that, "The plans are being prepared by Mr. Carpenter of New York and Mr. Robert H. Rheinlander of Glens Falls and are nearing completion. Mr. Rheinlander will have entire charge of building operations. Tools, equipment and materials are rapidly being assembled at Bolton, and the work is expected to proceed without interruption." The new clubhouse would feature one hundred rooms and fifty baths when opened in 1923.

Summer 1922, Sagamore Club Construction, from the back. Notice remains of Power Station on the left. (Courtesy, Gordon Garlick)

New Sagamore Club, November 10, 1922. (Courtesy, Gordon Garlick)

December 16, 1922. (Courtesy, Gordon Garlick)

1923, Early Spring. (Courtesy, Bolton Town Historian)

Sagamore Club, Spring 1923. (Courtesy, Bolton Town Historian)

The new Sagamore is a Georgian Colonial structure with its broad front porch facing the lake. Its design was borrowed from George Washington's home at Mount Vernon. The hotel opened for business on June 15th, 1923. The July 7th Lake George Mirror boasted, "The dreams and plans of many years have finally come true. The Sagamore is now a reality! The old hotel destroyed by fire in 1914 has been replaced by a new and fireproof clubhouse. The Sagamore has been formally opened under the direction of Burton F. White of New York, and is the newest of New York's summer recreation centers and one of the finest equipped establishments in the Adirondacks. It has been built in a way that it may be added to from time to time, having almost limitless space to build additional wings and sections without taking away from the general attractive appearance of its scenic and building features. Every convenience has been arranged for its patrons including garage facilities, a distinctive brand of good home cooking, motor boats and rowboats for recreation on the lake, eighteen well trained riding horses, and a transportation agreement with the Delaware and Hudson Company whereby the larger Lake George boats, the Horicon, Sagamore and Mohican, will make regular dock and train connections. Located as it is on the site of the old hotel, the present house has features from a scenic standpoint that are unrivaled. Entering through the north portal, one is in the lounge, a room thirty feet wide and fifty-four feet long. It has beams and pilasters and has a large fireplace at one end. While at the other end, beautifully carved and fluted pilasters mark the office entrances as well as the entrance to the ground floor rooms and baths, and a flight of stairs to the second story, all in the southwest wing.

Attractive gold and white electric fixtures of candle design are along the side walls, while suspended from the ceiling are hanging lights with the same gold and white decorative effect, creating an atmosphere of luxurious simplicity and comfort throughout the lounge. Heavy chenille rugs are laid over the hardwood floor in this room. As one stands in the lounge and looks to the south, a wide view of Lake George is visible through any of the five pairs of doors which open upon the south porch. This porch is sixteen feet wide and fifty-five long and two stories in height, the roof being supported by chaste columns twenty-four feet high and twenty inches in diameter. A large broad lawn graced with flower beds and foot paths runs down to the new concrete dock.

Leaving the lounge, one passes through the main stair hall at the right of which are writing rooms and entrance to the dining room in the southwest wing. This room has a clear span of thirty-six feet and length of fifty-eight feet, and is especially attractive with its double pilasters and its huge beams between which triple windows give views of the lake from three sides of the room. The dining room comfortably seats 150 persons. Attached to the dining room is a private or children's dining room, while beyond these are found pantries, servants' dining rooms and a kitchen thirty-one by thirty-four feet, this latter completely furnished with all the latest equipment and machinery. The kitchen and service rooms are in a wing at the northeast corner. The heating, refrigerating, water and storage plants are all in the basement.

The second and third floors are given over to guest rooms. The single, double and triple rooms all having baths and equipped with the finest fixtures. All the furnishings and equipment of the house, including the Wilton rugs with band borders, and the mahogany furniture in the bedrooms, three heavy Chenille rugs in the lounge and the cretonne that drapes all the windows, were furnished by Wilmarth & Son of Glens Falls."

Back of the new Sagamore Club, about 1924. (Courtesy, Ike Wolgin)

Front of the new Sagamore "Club", 1923.
(Courtesy, Henry Caldwell)

The summer seasons between 1923 and 1928 had their "ups and downs". By 1928, Dr. Beckers decided that new management might be just what the hotel needed to turn itself around. The stockholders agreed to hire famous hotelier Karl P. Abbott to supervise the management of the hotel. Karl Abbott said he was, "not interested in so small a place and that he could not afford to hire me to operate it, but I made him a sporting proposition. I said I'd run the club for one season on a bet, and if we make as much in that season as it lost the season before, you will have to build me a two-hundred-room hotel!" Mr. Abbott had never seen the hotel before so immediately he drove to Bolton Landing to check out his wager. "It was April, rainy and cold, and without getting out of the car I could see that the little clubhouse was not big enough to make any money out of rooms. We took up a French chef and started a party (catering) business and this, plus the rooms, made enough money to win my bet. That fall of 1929 I called on Dr. Beckers in New York. "When do we start building that hotel?" He was game. I engaged Harold Field Kellogg as architect, and we worked together forty-eight hours without stopping and completed a set of plans for a two-hundred room hotel. We wanted the building to appear as small as possible, so Kellogg designed it with four wings jutting from a common center. We broke ground on October 1, 1929. We began work with all the optimism in the world. The frame was up when the crash hit Wall Street. Dr. Beckers, who was hit hard during the crash, told me the hotel would have to wait. After the crash I found myself with nine hotels to carry (the Abbott Hotels Corporation) and another a third finished on Lake George." At this difficult time, Dr. Beckers convinced his longtime

friend, William H. Bixby of St. Louis and Mohican Point in Bolton, to finance the completion of the hotel. The Bixbys had just financed Charles Lindberg's trans-Atlantic flight on the "Spirit of St. Louis" in 1927. Dr. Beckers then, "transferred his interest in the hotel to the Essex Investment Co. of Saint Louis, which was owned by the Bixby family", according to Abbott. The construction work was completed by the Ormsby Brothers Construction Company of Bolton Landing. After the hotel was completed, there wasn't any money left to furnish it. Martin Wilmarth of Glens Falls came through with the furnishings just as the hotel was opening on July 1, 1930.

The New Tower, 1930.
(Courtesy, Bolton Historical Museum)

Abbott goes on to say, "We had 164 guests the first night, and the hotel was comfortably full for the remainder of the summer. We made a good profit that season, at the start of the Depression."

Dr. William G. Beckers
(Author's Collection)

William H. Bixby
(Courtesy, Doug Houghton)

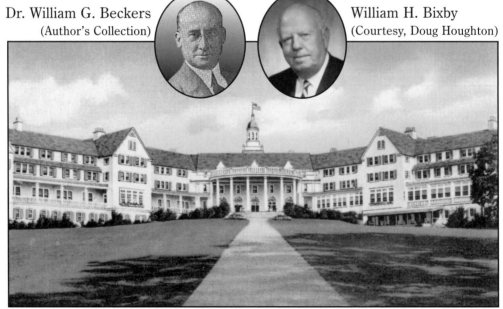

1930, Sagamore Hotel III completed. (Author's collection)

New 18 Hole Golf Course, 1928

While plans were being made during the 1920's to expand the Sagamore Club on Green Island into a hotel once again, it was generally agreed that a new 18 hole golf course was essential. John Boulton Simpson, as early as 1914, told the Glens Falls Times that, "Golf is the controlling influence these days that makes or breaks the success of every resort property, and his company must recognize this fact and equip themselves accordingly if they desire to attract neccessary patronage." In November of 1918, the Sagamore purchased the John Vandenburgh property, across from what is today Rogers Park in Bolton Landing, to be used as a golf course, however, soon afterward a more suitable property for a golf course was purchased on Federal Hill overlooking Lake George. On August 28, 1926, the Lake George Mirror stated that, "There has long been a demand for a golf course at the head of Lake George, and the Village of Lake George has discussed the subject on a good many occasions, but it remains for Bolton Landing to be the village to first put over such a course. It is planned to make an 18 hole course on this site. The site itself is one of the most beautiful that could be selected anywhere on the lake, for it overlooks Bolton and the Narrows, and commands a sweeping view of lake and mountains, both to the north and to the south."

The most qualified golf architect and engineer in the United States was hired to design the new links, Donald J. Ross of Pinehurst, North Carolina. Ross, the "patron saint of golf architecture," came to America from Dornoch, Scotland in 1899 with many golfing skills already to his credit. One year later he began his career as a golf architect, ready to help America meet its growing demand for new quality courses. The Mirror quotes Donald Ross as saying, "After careful inspection of the property on which it is proposed to construct an eighteen hole course, I am convinced that it has unusually fine possibilities for that purpose. The topography is gently rolling with very natural features which will add interest to the course. The soil is light, sandy loam, well suited for the production of a fine turf. From the plateau on which the property is located, approximately 800 feet above the level of Lake George, a magnificent view is open in all directions. In that respect, it is one of the most beautiful sites in the country."

Donald J. Ross,
Golf Architect.
(Author's Collection)

A July 16, 1927 Lake George Mirror said, "J. B. Cooper of Diamond Point, general contractor in charge of the work (on the golf course), expects to have the course completed and ready for play by June 1, 1928. Grading has been completed on nine holes, the fairways and greens of which are now ready for seeding. The design of the water supply and distributing system is in charge of E. M. Graff of Meyers, Bower and Ashley, Glens Falls. The reservoir will be supplied from local springs, and water is to be pumped from nearby ponds. Three miles of pipe will be used in the gravity distribution system.

A small clubhouse is planned to be erected this fall. This will be constructed at the highest point of the tract, which consists in the main of abandoned farms and timber lands. Dr. (William G.) Beckers stated today that the golf course is promoted by public spirited summer residents who desire to further the interests of the Bolton section." It should be noted that although it was named the Sagamore Golf Club, it was not owned at that time by the Sagamore Hotel, but by the corporation consisting of thirteen wealthy patrons. The 188 acre course, with 6,739 yards of fairway, was completed at a cost of $500,000 in 1928.

On Saturday, August 10, 1929, a house-warming celebration and golf match were held at the new Sagamore Golf Club House and Golf Course on Federal Hill. The Lake George Mirror said, "Approximately 400 people were present and this brilliant gathering watched the golf match with interest and enthusiasm. The exihibition game was played by J. J. O'Connor, the Sagamore Club pro, and Joe

The new Golf Club on Federal Hill, circa 1930.
Photo by Thatcher Studio, Pub. by T.J. Kennedy Co., Glens Falls. (Author's Collection)

Sagamore Golf Course (Club House in center).
Photo by Albertype Co. (Courtesy, Ike Wolgin)

Marzoitti, Lake George Club pro, and George Pulver of McGregor Club. Lord and Pulver defeated Marzoitti and O'Connor 2 up and 1 to play. The large gallery which accompanied the players was composed of many of the most prominent members of our summer colony and included Mrs. Sidney Homer, James Knapp, Miss Helen Simpson, Dr. and Mrs. Herbert Meyers, Adolph S. Ochs (Editor of the New York Times), Peter D. Kiernan, Dr. and Mrs. Edwin Jenks, Dr. William Beckers, Mr. William K. Bixby, Mr. Charles S. Peabody, Mr. Maurice Hoopes and Mr. Louis F. Hyde," to name a few.

Despite the crash of the Stock Market in 1929, the Great Depression of the 1930's and World War II, the golf course managed to remain open. The golf course was sold to the Sagamore hotel in 1938. The course was extremely popular in the second half of the twentieth century. The New York Times once called the Sagamore Golf Course, "One of the best ten in America."

During the early 1950's, Sagamore Golf "Pro" Joe Creavy and his brother Bill, were regular customers in my parents' Bill Gates Diner on Main Street in Bolton Landing. The Creavy brothers were nationally known golfers. The September 5, 1952 Post-Star said, "Joe Creavy, Pro at the Sagamore Golf Club, followed the tradition of his famous golf family when he hit his first hole-in-one recently. Joe's older brother Bill has two holes-in-one to his credit. His two other brothers, Tom and Jack have also at some time hit a hole-in-one".

Sagamore III "Amusements"

A SAGAMORE
PICNIC AT
PARADISE BAY

Photos from, *The Sagamore,* Karl Abbott.
(Courtesy, Bolton Historical Museum)

The Sagamore Horse Shows

A featured summer event, begun in August of 1934, was the Horse Show sponsored by the American Horse Show Association. Each three day event followed the resort circuit from Stockbridge, Mass. to Pittsfield, Mass. to the Sagamore in Bolton Landing and ended in Lake Placid. The 1937 show offered many prizes in the following catagories: Three-Gaited and Five-Gaited Saddlehorses, The Sagamore Hotel Challenge Trophy, The Bradley Challenge

From, *The Sagamore,* Karl P. Abbott.
(Courtesy, Bolton Historical Museum)

Trophy, Hunters, The Hall Challenge Trophy, Jumpers, Professional Horseman's Association Challenge Cup, The Kiernan Challenge Trophy, Camp Riding Competition Challenge Trophy, The Bradley Riding Stable Children's Challenge Trophy, Saddle Ponies for children under age 16, and Horsemanship. By 1940 there were sixty-two classes for the Seventh Annual "New Improved Show" which was held on August 8th, 9th and 10th. The July 18, 1940 Warrensburg News said, "Many junior riders from the summer camps in the Adirondacks provide spirited competition in the Junior classes."

To Exhibitors

- The Sagamore Horse Show will be held in the Outdoor Ring of The Sagamore Hotel, on each afternoon of August 6, 7, 8, excepting that a few classes will be started at 10:30 o'clock Saturday morning.

- The reservation of a box or parking space and the exhibition of your horses will materially assist us in making a success of our Fourth Annual Show.

- Applications for boxes and parking space will be filled in the order that they are received. As the number of either that are available is limited, applications for same should be mailed to the Secretary as early as possible.

- Boxes seating six persons $30.00. Ringside parking space for automobile $12.00 for the season (car and driver).

- Among the social events is an Exhibitors' dinner in the Main Dining room of the Sagamore Hotel, the Horse Show Ball held in the French Village and an evening on the renowned Lake George Show Boat.

- Entries close on July 28, 1937.

From, *Sagamore Horse Show,* Program, 1937.
(Courtesy, Henry Caldwell)

Prize Ribbon.
(Courtesy, Henry Caldwell)

Gold Cup Speedboat Races, 1934-1935-1936

During the summers of 1934, 1935, and 1936, the "World Champion Gold Cup Speedboat Races" arrived in Bolton Landing once again. Bolton's George Reis, and his racing boat "El Largarto", became champion in 1933 allowing him to select Lake George for the 1934 event. He won the championship two more times, attaining a speed of 72 mph, before he was finally defeated in 1936. Once again, the Sagamore Hotel was the focal point for the festivities surrounding the races which were sponsored by the Lake George (Yacht) Club.

Today, the "El Lagarto" is on permanent display at the Adirondack Museum in Blue Mountain Lake, New York.

"El Largarto" from Sagamore Dock, preparing for 1935 Gold Cup Races. Walter F. (Smokey) Gates, mechanic and George C. Reis, owner and driver. (Author's Collection)

Gold Cup Race, 1930's, "El Lagarto" at left. Photo from official 1936 Program.
(Author's collection)

Karl Abbott's, *The Sagamore,* advertised, "Your every wish has been anticipated at the Sagamore — a barber shop, beauty parlor, stock ticker, soda fountain, telephone and telegraph. The chambers, each with its private bath, with or without private parlor and private dining room ensuite, are all delightfully situated in that the hotel is built on the plan of a cross, all rooms being outside rooms with a pleasant outlook. (Lake George) is the most beautiful lake in America."

Early Aerial View — Notice oval horse show track on former golf course.
Photo by Tichnor Bros. (Courtesy, Richard & Mary Kowell)

Sagamore III, Circa 1939. Photo by Tichnor Bros.
(Courtesy, Richard & Mary Kowell)

Aerial View, circa early 1940's. Photo by Lumitone Photoprint
(Author's Collection)

Open Veranda. Photo by Albertype Co.
(Courtesy, Ike Wolgin)

Former Lighthouse on pier, and flag signaling steamboat to land.
Photo by Albertype Co. (Courtesy, Ike Wolgin)

The Tea Terrace, from *The Sagamore,* Karl P. Abbott.
(Courtesy, Bolton Historical Museum)

The Sagamore Docks, facing Bolton Landing. Steamboat *Mohican II* approaching. Photo by Albertype Co. (Author's collection)

The Swimming Docks. Photo by Albertype Co.
(Courtesy, Author's Collection)

Waterspout

(Tornado) off the Sagamore Dock — On July 20, 1945 a funnel, between 50 to 100 feet wide and 1,500 to 2,000 feet high and lasting approximately 10 minutes, traveled from north of Dome Island, very close to the Sagamore dock and into Northwest Bay where it disappeared. An extremely rare sight on Lake George!

Photo by Clara Smith. (This copy courtesy, Ted Rehm & Gordon Garlick)

The Swimming Docks. Photo by Albertype Co.
(Courtesy, Author's Collection)

A Children's Party — "The Sagamore is the ideal resort for children. Its spacious lawns and woodlands, interspersed with winding paths, make an ideal playground. A children's indoor playroom is provided." From *The Sagamore,* Karl P. Abbott.
(Courtesy, Bolton Historical Museum)

The Lounge — Photo by Albertype Co.
(Author's Collection)

Fireplace in Early
American Grill — *The
Sagamore,* Karl P. Abbott.
(Courtesy, Bolton
Historical Museum)

Dining Room —
Photo by Albertype Co.
(Courtesy, Ike Wolgin)

The French Village Grill — Photo by Albertype Co.
(Courtesy, Gordon Garlick)

Sagamore III – After World War II

The Karl Abbott years at the Sagamore were relatively successful ones considering that the Great Depression and World War II negatively affected the vacation climate in America during that same fifteen year period from 1930 to 1945. The September 14, 1944 Glens Falls Times reported that Mr. Abbott was pleased with the summer's business. The Times said, "This year for the first time the Sagamore operated on a club basis, even the name of the resort being changed (again) from the "Sagamore Hotel" (to the Sagamore Club) to carry out the transition. Guests have all been members of the club, passed upon by a membership committee, and more than 6,000 are listed. Evidence of the Sagamore's popularity among the nation's leading businessmen is found in the fact that several wartime conferences have been conducted there. Mr. Abbott will remain at the Sagamore until October 15th when he and Mrs. Abbott and their younger son, Karl, will leave for Florida to spend the winter at the (Abbott) Trade Winds Club".

In Karl Abbott's book, *Open for the Season,* he wrote, "For fifteen happy years I ran the Sagamore. My family spent the summer there and wintered in the south. The dozen or so other hotels I ran in those years were fun, and I was having a wonderful time. A few hours' sleep at night, a cat nap during the day, kept me fit."

In April of 1946, the Sagolf Corporation purchased the Sagamore Hotel and Golf Course. Sagolf, owned by the Brandt brothers, was a subsidiary of Brandt Enterprises which owned a chain of movie theaters from New York City to Florida, as well as Camp Arcady children's camp on Lake George, and the Scaroon Manor Hotel on Schroon Lake in the Adirondacks. Louis Brandt purchased "Villa Nirvana" and made it his summer home.

Louis Brandt,
(Photo by Mark Frost, 1982.
Courtesy, The Chronicle)

The Brandts had purchased the Sagamore for a definite reason. It had discriminated against their family a few seasons earlier by not encouraging their patronage because they were Jewish. After the purchase, this problem was immediately corrected – the hotel, managed by James Fayko, now catered primarily to Jewish guests, and continued to do so for many years to follow. Many of the new guests came from the entertainment world.

Among the improvements Brandt added to the hotel were indoor and outdoor swimming pools, a nightclub, and a gate at the entrance to the island, the latter reportedly installed to give Mr. Brandt some modest protection for his Saturday night poker games held at "Wapanak".

Outdoor Swimming Pool on Lawn was ten feet deep. Notice indoor pool is not yet constructed at left. Photo by Richard K. Dean. (Author's Collection)

Outdoor Pool. *MV Ticonderoga* leaving the pier, 1950's.
Photo by Richard K. Dean. (Author's Collection)

To the left of the hotel, Brandt added the separate indoor pool building where
"Belle View" once stood. At right, "Wapanak" stands alone on the treeless shore.
Photo by Richard K. Dean. (Author's Collection)

Sagamore in Winter, 1950's. Crown Island in background.
Photo by Richard K. Dean. (Author's Collection)

Governors' Conference, 1954

On July 11 - 14, 1954, the 46th Annual United States Governors' Conference was held at the Sagamore Hotel. According to the original program for the annual conference, "The Governors Have Developed a New Instrument (the conference) for Perfecting The Union of The States." As a nine year old youngster, I can clearly recall the exciting arrival of Richard Nixon's motorcade as he waved to us from a black convertible. New York's veteran Governor Thomas E. Dewey hosted the event at the Sagamore. Dan Thornton, Governor of Colorado, was chairman. All forty-eight governors were in attendance. President Dwight D. Eisenhower was scheduled to be the keynote speaker, however, at the last moment he was unable to attend due to the death of his sister-in-law, Mrs. Milton Eisenhower. Vice President Richard Nixon took his place. It was also exciting for me, and my friends, to see the forty-eight heavily guarded blue and yellow-gold Ford automobiles assembled on the Bolton Ball Field which were provided to each governor by the Ford Motor Company. After the convention, these Fords were converted for use by the New York State Police Department.

The convention consisted of over 300 participants — 97 news reporters, the 48 governors with their wives and staff members, and a platoon of New York State Troopers to assist the FBI with security. Louis Brandt received much praise for the Sagamore's contribution toward the success of the convention. He had made many major improvements to the hotel and its grounds to ensure that success, such as, new wall-to-wall carpeting, an air-conditioned television lounge, and many new flowers and shrubs. Also, a news center was established for the press to quickly and conveniently report to the nation. Governor Dewey personally selected the Sagamore Hotel as the site for the convention so the nation's governors, and the world, could see the exceptional beauty of Lake George and New York State. Frank Leonbruno's book, *Lake George Reflections,* speaks best for all of us from Bolton when he says, "The convention was truly the affair of the century for our little town. It will be remembered as the event which brought unparalleled publicity to the region, as the eyes of the nation were focused on Bolton Landing and Lake George for those four glorious days in July of 1954."

1954 — New York Governor, Thomas E. Dewey & Vice President, Richard M. Nixon at the Sagamore.
(Photo by Richard K. Dean)

Commemorative Ashtray – designed and produced
by Alfred University's Ceramics Department.
(Courtesy, Bolton Historical Museum)

Richard Nixon at the
Sagamore Golf Course, 1954.
(Photo by Richard K. Dean.
Courtesy, The Chronicle)

Sagamore Golf Course on Federal Hill, 1960's. Green Island, above left.
(Photo by Richard K. Dean)

Sagamore Hotel on Green Island, 1968. Islands of the Narrows in background.
(Photo by Richard K. Dean)

DEC Headquarters on Green Island, 1962 to Present.
(Photo by Author)

Visitors to Green Island are often curious about a large complex of green buildings along the island's northwest shore. During 1962, the New York State Environmental Conservation Department purchased this property from Philip and Aletha Walker to construct their new Lake George headquarters. During an earlier time period, this land had been owned by George O. Knapp of Shelving Rock, Ernest Granger and Albert Judson for the purpose of boat storage. The DEC at 18 Boathouse Lane now consists of several boat houses, workshops, offices and storage facilities. Eventually, it also became the headquarters for the lake's picnic and camping islands, and the primary storage and maintenance area for navigational aids and buoys for the entire lake. The driving force behind this acquisition, its funding and construction was Victor Glider, who was DEC's Director of Lands and Forests.

DEC Headquarters. (Photo by Author)

Sagamore III – 1981 to the Present

The 1960's and 1970's brought few changes to the Sagamore. It opened for business every season with relatively good success, then routinely closed every winter as it had always done in the previous one-hundred years of its history. In the meantime, the Adirondack Northway (I-87) had been constructed during the late 1960's providing downstate and Canadian visitors with a significantly easier access to Lake George. With many modern motels rapidly being constructed around the lake, and with only modest amounts of money being spent to maintain the hotel, business at the Sagamore began falling off by the end of the 1970's. The final blow arrived in the fall of 1980 when Louis Brandt was notified that an extensive amount of renovations were now required to upgrade the hotel to meet new fire prevention regulations. Unwilling to make these expenditures, Brandt decided not to open the hotel for the 1981 season. Like a friendly neighbor who is greatly missed after he is gone, Bolton Landing's summer of 1981 didn't feel quite the same with the hotel sitting silently over on the island.

During the summer of 1981, summer residents Norman and Marian Wolgin of Philadelphia, along with their son Ike, often passed by the empty hotel in their boat, and soon they began discussing its possibilities. By November of 1981, Norman Wolgin had signed a sale contract with Sagolf President Louis Brandt. After nearly one entire year of negotiations, the sale was completed for the hotel and golf course in September of 1982 for $5,000,000. Louis Brandt's thirty-five year association with the Sagamore Hotel was now in the past.

The first order of business by the new owners was to place the hotel on the National Register of Historic Places. In June of 1983, the Sagamore opened a week-long sale where thousands of people purchased more than 50,000 items through the National Content Liquidators of Dayton, Ohio.

Sagamore Liquidation Sale, June 1983.
(Photo by Beth Wright for the Glens Falls Post-Star)

A memorable "Ground Breaking Celebration" was held on the Sagamore's front lawn on July 17, 1983. All of the residents of Bolton were invited to share in the festivites by attending the large lawn party. My daughter Allison, who was eight years old at the time, came along with me to enjoy the history, people, food, beverages and live rock and roll band. The weather that day was warm and sunny — perfect. When we left, we were all given commemorative glass mugs for souvenirs of that historic day.

Ground Breaking Souvenir.
(Courtesy, Dawn K. Gates)

Norman Wolgin and the Kennington Corporation of Los Angeles gutted the hotel and added insulation with the plan to open the hotel year round. The original 200 rooms were modified into 110 rooms and luxury suites. Although the interior was extensively changed, the colonial designed exterior was consistently maintained. An 800 seat convention center was added along with a new indoor swimming pool building which was attached to the hotel. There were also new tennis courts, an indoor sports facility, an exercise center, health spa, raquetball court, jogging trail, children's playground and several new restaurants. A large reception center was built on the island immediately after crossing the bridge. The 18 hole, 188 acre golf course was totally restored using Donald Ross's original plans as a guide, featuring natural hogback greens, Ross designed bunkers, and wide fairways. It is irrigated with an underground sprinkler system.

240 rooms were added to the complex in the form of "cottages" on the first floor, with condominium units on the second and third levels. Dock facilities were greatly expanded along the island's west shoreline, north of the bridge. The original 1883 stable and carriage house was renovated into "The Hermitage", a retreat for executives with its own board room, dining room and ten luxury suites, each with its own bar and private garden.

After being closed for four years, the hotel reopened on June 7, 1985 with its $75,000,000 restoration project mostly completed. For the next ten years it was operated by the Omni Hotels Management Company as a four-star resort. Today, the hotel is self-managed and employs approximately 750 people during the summer months and 240 during the winter.

Throughout 1985 and the spring of 1986, another project had begun on Green Island in the Sagamore's warehouse on Boathouse Lane. Bill Morgan of Morgan Marine had begun construction on the Sagamore's new 72 foot cruise boat

"Morgan" which the hotel had named for him. With a lifelong interest in boats and history, I often visited and photographed the construction site. I was fortunate to become her captain during her exciting maiden summer of 1986.

The hull is made from plywood reinforced with layers of fiberglass. She is powered by a single diesel driven propeller. The Morgan is capable of carrying 150 people, with dining facilities for 85.

"The Morgan"

The Morgan's hull – launched July 17, 1985 from Sagamore's warehouse.
(Photo by Evelyn Hersh)

The Morgan under construction – Fall 1985.
(Photo by Author)

The Morgan – Her first summer, 1986.
(Photo by Author)

"Villa Nirvana" – *The Morgan* – The Sagamore Hotel. (Summer 2000)
(Photo by Author)

The Sagamore Hotel today.
(Photo by Richard K. Dean)

1930 Concrete Bridge received wooden facade in 1985 which was removed during the bridge's renovation in the spring of 2001. (Both photos by Author)

118

Bridge Restoration. Spring 2001. (Photo by Author)

Helen Simpson's Playhouse. Now owned by the Gabriels family. Porch enclosed, a small addition built, and bark siding replaced with shingles in 1935. Placed on National Register of Historic Places in 1983. (Photo by Author) (See page 21)

The 1883 Stable and Carriage Barn is now "The Hermitage". (See page 30)
(Photo by Author)

Reception Center and Registration Building, 2001. (Photo by Author)

The Condominiums and First Floor Cottages, 2001.
(Photos by Author)

120

The Sagamore Today. (Photo by Dick Kowell)

The Sagamore and Tower today.
(Photo by Richard K. Dean)

The Tower, 1930's.
Photo by Albertype Co.
(Courtesy, Henry Caldwell)

Epilogue

When the Industrial Revolution began in the latter 1800's, the world, as we knew it, rapidly changed. Although the Adirondack region earns its livelihood primarily from the tourist trade, we too have lived through significant changes here on Lake George. Back when the Sagamore was in its early years, there were nearly 25 hotels around the lake, each offering luxury, comfort, entertainment and beauty to those early travelers who were willing to strike out into the wilderness which was once this region. Today, these grand establishments are gone — most of their manicured grounds have been subdivided and developed, however Lake George is still here with us to quietly enjoy and to preserve — and we are very fortunate to have so much of our pristine natural shoreline owned and protected by the State of New York. My family, who has lived here in Bolton since 1790, has passed down to us through the generations, a strong appreciation and respect for Lake George, the mountains, the boats, the people and the rich history that surrounds us. The Sagamore symbolizes all of these. It is a magnificent monument to all who built it and to all who have vacationed there, and dreamed there, since 1883. Like Uncas, in Cooper's, "Last of the Mohicans", the Sagamore is the last of the grand hotels still in existence here on Lake George.

William Preston Gates
Spring, 2001

$\mathcal{B}ibliography$

Abbott, K. *Open for the Season*. Garden City, New York: Doubleday & Company, Inc., 1950.

Abbott, K. *The Sagamore, Lake George, NY.* Bolton Landing, New York. (Pamphlet)

Bolton, Town of. *Bolton Bicentennial Calendar*. Bolton Landing, New York, 1998. (Calendar)

[1] Brown, M. O. *The Sagamore, Lake George*. Bolton Landing, New York, 1889. (Pamphlet)

Brown, M. O. *The Sagamore*. Bolton Landing, New York, 1893.

Brown, M. O. *The Sagamore, Green Island, Lake George*. Bolton Landing, New York, 1894.

Brown, M. O. *The Sagamore, Lake George*. Bolton, Landing, New York, 1895.

Brown, M. O. *The Sagamore, Green Island, Lake George*. Bolton Landing, New York, 1899.

Buckell, B. *Old Lake George Hotels*. Lake George, New York: Buckle Press, 1986.

Chronicle, The. (Newspaper) Glens Falls, New York.

Delaware and Hudson Co. *A Summer Place*. Albany, New York: The Passenger Department, The D&H Company, 1913.

French's Gazetteer. (Geographical Dictionary) 1861.

Gates, W. P. *Turn-of-the-Century Scrapbook of Jonathan Streeter Gates*. Glens Falls & Bolton, New York: Gates Publishing Company, 1999.

Glens Falls Star. (Newspaper)

Glens Falls Times. (Newspaper)

Halm, G. and Sharp, M. *Images of America, Lake George*. Charleston, South Carolina: Arcadia Publishing, 2000.

[2] Krumbholz, T. E. *The Sagamore on Lake George*. Sagamore, New York. (Pamphlet)

Lake George Mirror. (Newspaper)

Leonbruno, F. *Lake George Reflections, Island History and Lore*. Fleischmanns, New York: Purple Mountain Press, 1998.

O'Brien, K. *The Great and the Gracious on Millionaires' Row*. Sylvan Beach, New York: North Country Books, 1978.

Possons, C. *Possons Guide to Lake George, Lake Champlain and Adirondacks*. Glens Falls, New York: Chas. H. Possons, Publisher, 1893.

Post-Star, The. (Newspaper)

Stoddard, S. R. *Lake George Illustrated*. Glens Falls, New York, 1886.

Stoddard, S .R. *Lake George and Lake Champlain, A Book of Today*. Glens Falls, New York, 1891.

Stoddard, S. R. *Saratoga, Lake George and Lake Champlain*. Glens Falls, New York, 1905.

Stoddard, S. R. *Lake George and Lake Champlain, A Book of Today*. Glens Falls, New York, 1910.

Stoddard, S. R. *Lake George and Lake Champlain, A Book of Today*. Glens Falls, New York, 1914.

Tippetts, W. *Lake George and Surroundings*. Caldwell, New York, 1901.

Warrensburg(h) News. (Newspaper)

Lake George

Loch Lomond's depths are dusky brown,
   Purple her hills with heather;
From shore to shore her bare peaks frown
   In mild and stormy weather.

Green are the slopes of Windermere,
   All pure her limpid waters.
A liquid gem without a peer
   To Britain's sons and daughters.

But thou art all, oh, lake of lakes!
   Lake George, thou art unequalled;
Thy beetling crags the storm-cloud breaks;
   With elves thine isles are peopled.

The mighty eagle rests his wing
   Where rear thy rocky shoulders,
The tiniest harebells shyly cling
   Among thy shore-bound boulders.

As in a boat I rock and swing,
   By summer scenes enraptured,
No lake the old world poets sing
   Has thus my senses captured.

From, *Possons' Guide to Lake George, Lake Champlain and Adirondacks* by Chas. H. Possons, Publisher, Glens Falls, NY, in 1893.
(Courtesy, Henry Caldwell)

Another Best-Selling Book by Bill Gates

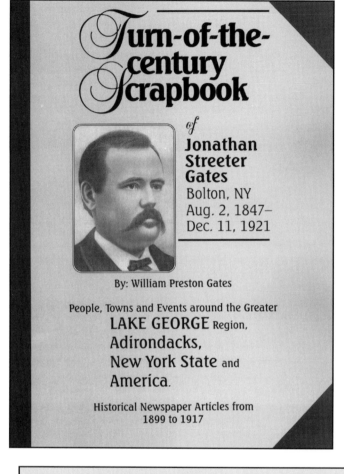